OUTSIDE

Poetry and Prose

André du Bouchet

Selected, Translated, and Presented

by

Eric Fishman and Hoyt Rogers

BITTER OLEANDER
P R E S S
2020

The Bitter Oleander Press
4983 Tall Oaks Drive
Fayetteville, New York 13066-9776
USA
www.bitteroleander.com

André du Bouchet, *Outside*:

ISBN #978-0-9993279-8-2

Library of Congress Control Number: 2020931765

Layout and Design by Roderick Martinez

Cover art: Gilles du Bouchet, casein collage on paper, made especially for the cover, from the artist's collection, 10.5 x 26 cm (2020)

Back cover: a facsimile from one of André du Bouchet's notebooks (1951)

Manufactured in the United States of America

———— ✦ ————

ACKNOWLEDGMENTS

Translation, as its etymology tells us, is an act of "carrying over"; with moral or practical support, various friends and relatives have helped us convey these poems from French to English, and we would like to thank them here. Above all, we owe a debt of gratitude to Anne de Staël, for her generous permission to reprint and translate her late husband's work, as well as to the poet's son, Gilles du Bouchet, for the cover artwork. Paul Auster, the earliest translator of du Bouchet's poetry, read the manuscript with care and offered a number of valuable comments. We must also acknowledge Paul B. Roth, the founder of The Bitter Oleander Press, for his patient editorial guidance. Clément Layet helped us obtain facsimiles from du Bouchet's notebooks. Along the way, Sarah Plimpton, John Taylor, Peter Cole, and Philippe Blanc—among many others—kindly came to our aid.

Eric Fishman's translations "Varengeville" and "Dry life" originally appeared in *The Bitter Oleander*, Fall 2018; "Notebook fragments, 1952-1954" was first published in AGNI Online, February 2019; "Waltz/Marine," "Repetition," and "A cow that coughs in the fog..." appeared in *Exchanges*, Fall 2019; "Before the whiteness" was published in *Eunoia Review*, December 2019; and "Motor of Night," in *Cortland Review,* May 2020.

Hoyt Rogers's translation "Letter" first appeared in *Poetry*, October-November 2000; "The Journey" was published in *Cerise Press*, Fall 2013; "Dawn without sun" and "Mist gently smothers sight" appeared in *Plume Poetry*, August 2019; "Englargement" was published in *AGNI*, October 2019; "The City, the field, burning soundless..." and "Another Recourse" appeared in *The Bitter Oleander,* Spring, 2020.

All these reviews deserve a special word of thanks for their ongoing commitment to literary translation.

Finally, we wish to express our deep appreciation to Mercure de France, Fata Morgana, Gallimard, and Le Bruit du temps—du Bouchet's forward-looking publishers in France—for allowing us to reproduce and translate his work. Detailed information about the copyrights they hold is furnished in the Source Notes at the end of this book.

CONTENTS

Translated by Eric Fishman o
Translated by Hoyt Rogers *

The Poetic Geology of André du Bouchet

upright on great sediments of world...

André du Bouchet (1924-2001) was one of the major poets, translators, and critics of late twentieth century France. Yet the first time we encounter his poetry, we may feel bewildered. Particularly in his later poems, the lines are taken over by white space, the marks vanishing into the void of the page. And the text that remains seems to lack narrative, protagonists, and — perhaps most jarringly for an Anglophone reader — emotion. What's happening? And how does the speaker feel about it? Du Bouchet turns away from our questions, and instead shows us objects: the mountains, water, a window. As poet and critic Yves Bonnefoy noted in an early review: "An aspect of André du Bouchet's work that never fails to surprise us, and sometimes to frighten us… is the absence of that voice of confession or confidence which we have decided, since Romanticism no doubt, to identify with poetry."

Du Bouchet denies the reader a subjective standpoint from which to understand his writing. He disclaims any interest in his feelings, or even his own words. Instead, he's searching for something he considers more fundamental. As he notes in a poetic essay on his craft:

> It's now a matter of depersonalization, in order to move outside [*dehors*]… I'm looking for something other than my expression … Something other than myself … in order to begin with the world.

Dehors. Outside. Du Bouchet eschews the usual poetic dialogue of self and reality: instead of external events or intimate thoughts, we confront what my fellow translator Hoyt Rogers has called a "drama of description." The narrative is driven by a process of perception, an effort to construct "the mountain in *reality*, once whoever drew it is removed."

> Like the field that flows toward the wide-open fence where it stops, while the sun, at the end of day, floods us with its ice, and disappears.
>
> But all this time, in the crystalline air, the stubborn forehead of the fence, if possible, draws nearer …

The poet is still present, but only as a recipient of the sensations that overtake him as he walks. Though the ice of sunset floods toward him, the fence remains the focus of these stanzas; the boundary-line of the field becomes the horizon of observation. The barrier's "forehead" approaches the poet: the object has been transmuted into a subject.

This rhythm of walking, with external features entering the field of vision only to disappear, structures much of du Bouchet's poetry. In the course of his life, he filled over one hundred and fifty notebooks with fragments he jotted down during long rambles through the wheat fields of Vexin, the streets of Paris, and the snowy landscapes of Truinas. Many such annotations are included in *Outside*, derived from transcriptions made by the scholar Clément Layet. The reader will also find poems du Bouchet composed decades later from the "ore" of his notebooks, dissected and reassembled using "[blank] pages, a typewriter, scissors, glue, and a drawing board."

This collage-like method, which du Bouchet employed for several of his later collections (*Notebook*, *Notebook 2*, and *Notebook 3*), provides a window on the inner workings of his poetics. His poems themselves proceed much like a collage artist sifting through a box of scraps — picking up, examining, and piecing together impressions that almost seem to elude his outstretched hands. "My poem runs ceaselessly / in front of me ..."

We are guided along du Bouchet's train of thought by an ambiguous use of punctuation that echoes, at times, Emily Dickinson's characteristic dashes:

> poppies,
> the red harvest — ripe tomatoes, rather, and silence
> under my sole

The line halts, and one image of bountiful red is replaced by another. The em-dash functions like the momentary flicker between frames in a film. The phrases are juxtaposed, snapshots of the same scene viewed from different angles: poppies, tomatoes. What emerges is a composite, a three-dimensional image formed by fragments.

Yet "train of thought" may not be the right metaphor for du Bouchet's trajectory, as it implies lateral movement toward a destination. More frequently, he takes a vertical approach. The poem progresses from the objects around him (poppies, tomatoes) toward what is underfoot (silence). He strives to fracture the surface of what's immediately visible, wielding the "eye / [as] a switch-blade."

This sense of excavation is most striking when du Bouchet discusses geological formations, depicting them in remarkably technical terms.

> across from me, the
> quarry empty today on the mountainside — a scarring
>
> base of the synclines, abrupt torsion of overlapping
> rocky parallels

Geology serves the poet as a metaphor for language. The sediment of words, deposited through daily use, is compressed and distorted by the pressure and heat of time to shape the striations of language, the poet's quarry. However, du Bouchet's poems resemble industrial mining less than a natural process of weathering. His stanzas gradually wear away the layers in order to expose what's underneath: perhaps "the muffled, crackling breath of the ancient word" – or the silence of the blank page.

As with metamorphic rock, du Bouchet's poems frequently mold language into surprising formations. Conventions of syntax bend, referents give way, and we suddenly notice that "the sentence is shattered." As readers, we are constantly reminded of the imperfections of language; his poems point toward the tenuous relationship between words and what they seek to describe:

> *rauschen*   word for a sound outside language

This may explain why the act of translation is central to du Bouchet's work — and not just because he himself was a prolific translator, working with texts as varied as those of Faulkner, Shakespeare, Joyce, Mandelstam, Pasternak, Hölderlin, and Celan. Translation is an ideal site for du Bouchet to explore what happens when language breaks down. The disorientation we experience as readers of his work is what he intends. By obliging us to step outside our comfortable relationship with words, he allows us to encounter them anew.

> in language
>
> as from the other side of language

Early on, du Bouchet underwent a visceral estrangement from French. He was born in Paris in 1924 to a family of Russian Jewish and French American ancestry, but he and his parents escaped to Boston in 1940, fleeing the Nazi invasion. Though he finally returned to Paris eight years later, he never quite shook off the impression of being a foreigner in his own language. Yet it was precisely this distance that enabled him to examine French with the acuity of an outsider.

> keep something of the
> uninhabited threshold in the language once you've entered in.

For English-speaking readers, the pieces in *Outside* expand the access to du Bouchet offered by *Openwork*, the selection published by Paul Auster and Hoyt Rogers in 2014; deliberately, none of those texts is repeated here. Like the earlier volume, *Outside* affords a cross-section of du Bouchet's vast and highly varied work: from the dreamlike landscapes of his youthful poems to the mineral shards of his later compositions, which waver between poetry and prose. Even more than *Openwork*, *Outside* places a particular emphasis on the lyrical fragments from du Bouchet's notebooks. All the texts in this new collection follow the chronological order of their original publication— or in the case of the notebook entries, their date of composition—and all have been rendered into English for the first time. Du Bouchet's oeuvre is immense, and much of it still remains untranslated.

Many of du Bouchet's works first appeared in large formats. Because of limitations of scale or space, some of the following selections have necessarily been reduced in length. While this applies more often to the notebook entries, which were never in a finalized state, a few of the more voluminous printed texts have also been compressed. Not only did du Bouchet adopt this technique in revising his own poems and notebook entries for later publications, but he also employed it in editing a collection of Victor Hugo's work. The Source Notes indicate which pieces have been distilled.

Du Bouchet's poetry has sometimes been misjudged as obscure. On the contrary, a careful reading of his works reveals that they are structured around observations of the physical world. More than with most authors, English renderings of du Bouchet need to draw on the concrete Germanic roots of our language, as opposed to their more abstract Latinate counterparts. Priority must always be given to what is signified by his lines—*a sense for sense* translation, or perhaps even a *thing for thing* translation—as opposed to word-for-word equivalents. This reflects du Bouchet's own methods as a translator. As he asserted:

> I translated —
> to put down again, what was outside the book
> and isn't a word.

Like his originals, translations of du Bouchet's work must seek a language dense with objects; placed along the blank expanse of the page, his words are like stones the reader can hold up to the light.

— *Eric Fishman*

OUTSIDE

Valse

La valse-océan
Dont les cordes meurent dans le vent
Se déchaîne dans les remous
et les manigances du vent
Au bout du port un homme gesticule
Comme une hélice brisée
Le grand espace se renverse
et nous frôle
on va tout recommencer

Marine

Parages ou tu t'installes comme un citron dans un miroir. De faux visages familiers
se renversent en porte-à-faux, déferlent et se recoupent dans les embruns acides,
sucrés, acides, dont tu te défais en glissant dans une vague chargée de filaments
et d'ailerons en biseau vers la patrie des coquillages.

Waltz

Strings dying in the wind
The ocean-waltz
Unchains itself in the schemes
and eddies of the wind
At the edge of the harbor a man gestures
Like a broken propeller
The vast space is upended
and brushes past us
everything begins again

Marine

Waters where you settle like a lemon in a mirror. Sham familiar faces awkwardly
capsize, break and crisscross in sour, sweet, sour spray that you escape by
sliding into a wave teeming with threads and beveled fins toward the land
of shellfish.

« La chrysalide »

La chrysalide.

      Bientôt nous allons habiter dans les arbres. Jardin grand
Meaulnes. Chambres frissons d'eau —
Alors, « trop fin », dit-on.
J'ai assez de rudesse et d'orgueil pour suffire —
      d'adresse pour ménager le temps.
   du premier coup…
draps, aube, et couverture
   renvoyés en boule

(la nuit ne desserre pas son accueil. Ses ombelles couleur de poussière et
d'anis. Nuit rauque. Un million de fourmis dans les talons. Si claire et si
vide, ouverte à tel point qu'on éclate de rire). — Ne pas tant se soucier
de former un tout cohérent — d'accoler les phares.

  dans la volière
      homme du départ
chavire dans l'intervalle
quelle noyade —
         trop parfait.

Parfois, j'ai mes raisons d'écrire. Cela suffit ; peu importe
ce qui s'ensuit
     carreaux de feuilles losanges d'eau
     cheveux du vent
     un éclair blanc résonne
     dans les volets une seule lucarne à vif
     on déplace les meubles de la nuit.

     ouverte à tout mot venant
     (qui s'échappe des lèvres comme une bulle)

     Le silence à petits coups de marteau
     nous voilà paré pour l'échafaud —
     d'autre part   les métros de l'aurore
     le pain joyeux
     les boîtes à lettres azur
        mouches, mouches…

'The chrysalis'

The chrysalis.

       Soon we'll be living in the trees. A Grand Meaulnes garden.
Rooms quivering with water —
And so, 'too refined,' they say.
I have gruffness and pride enough to spare —
          and skill to husband time.
     right off the bat...
sheets, dawn, and bedcovers
  thrown off in a ball.

(the night doesn't dwindle its welcome. Its umbels the color of dust and aniseed. Hoarse night. A million ants in the heels. So bright and empty, open so wide you burst out laughing.) — Don't worry too much about shaping a coherent whole — about stringing phrases together.

  in the birdcage
         departing man
keels over in the interim
what a drowning —
        too perfect.

Sometimes, I have my reasons for writing. That's enough; it doesn't much matter what follows
        panes of leaves rhombuses of water
        hairs of wind
        a white thunderbolt resounds
        in the shutters a single light on edge
        night's furniture is moved.

        open to any word that comes along
        (that escapes the lips like a bubble)

        Silence with little hammer-strokes
        and we're dressed for the scaffold —
        on the other hand   the subways of dawn
        the joyous bread
        the mailboxes sky-blue
            flies, flies...

Le rôle des mots

        suivre une ligne
parallèle à
      et donner l'illusion
        bienfaisante
d'accompagner la respiration.
   (non de la remplacer, toute
  réflexion faite.)

les impondérables : air,
circulation, respiration, etc.

Trop raréfié
   retrouver le goût
de la violence physique.

The role of words

        follow a line
parallel to
      and give the nurturing
          illusion
of moving together with breath.
      (not replacing it, everything
considered.)

the imponderables: air,
circulation, breathing, etc.

Too rarefied
      recover the taste
of physical violence.

Moteur de la nuit

Le ciel en brèche

L'eau n'a pas encore eu le temps de sécher
elle s'étale sur la chaussée
comme une main

      Nuage en marche

Il n'y a pas de vent
il n'y a pas de lumière

      Nuit
      souffle coupé

Chien à ramper vers l'ombre
À souffler sur la poussière avec le museau
Dans l'étoffe froide du matin

Une aile détachée roule dans le ciel

Les nuages plus vifs que la pierre
déboulent de la gorge et brisent leurs amarres
Ils lapident le ciel

Le jour qui renaît me porte doucement à terre

La poitrine vorace creusant toujours le ciel
l'œil
au cran d'arrêt
Je fais la monnaie de la lumière.

Motor of night

Ruptured sky

The water hasn't had time to dry
it spreads on the road
like a hand

        Cloud on the move

There's no wind
there's no light

        Night
        breathless

Dog crawling toward the shadow
Breathing on the dust with its muzzle
In the morning's cold weave

An unfastened wing rolls in the sky

Clouds sharper than stone
tumble from the throat and break their moorings
They stone the sky

Reborn day brings me gently to earth

The insatiable chest still mining the sky
the eye
a switch-blade
I make coins from light.

Répétition

TOUT A ÉTÉ DIT
    MAIS IL FAUT SANS CESSE LE RÉPETÉR
                        comme on respire

alors en le répétant
          en tordant la plume

    « les taies tombent »

et l'air qui entre par la fenêtre ouverte
      remue la maison comme un drap

on ne voit pas les autres étoiles

      il n'y a que ce grand couvercle de verre
cet œil brouillé de nuages

on est bien à terre
            amarré par le vent
     les câbles du versant
le monde qui se déroule
            la route et le corbeau
                     le jour
                     chauffant
                     le pourtour
                     de l'œil

Repetition

EVERYTHING HAS BEEN SAID
    BUT MUST BE CEASELESSLY REPEATED
                                like breathing

so by repeating
            by twisting the pen

    'the scales fall'

and the air coming through the open window
        shakes the house like a sheet

we don't see the other stars

        there's nothing but this huge lid of glass
this cloud-blurred eye

we're firmly on the ground
                moored by the wind
        the cables on the cliff
the world unfolding
            the road and the raven

                        the day
                        warming
                        the rim
                        of the eye

Fragments de cahier, avril 1951

Horreur de voir ces choses *se composer* en mots.

Deux poètes, deux poésies :
celle qui emboîte : celle qui s'élabore tandis que le héros reste muet, les mots
du silence, celle qui emboîte la parole au héros.

      le poème redevient sourd aveugle muet
      l'homme

                  mort

Sonnette du rémouleur,
trille, battement d'ailes dans les arbres
et la *rumeur immense* des voitures.
Je suis celui qui voit et qui écoute.

Nuit ou jour, tout est vue, vie.

Notebook fragments, April 1951

Horror of seeing these things *compose themselves* into words.

Two poets, two poetries:
one that takes form while the hero doesn't speak, the words
of silence, one that links together the hero's words.

.

      the poem becomes deaf blind mute once again
      the man

                dead

Bell of the knife-grinder,
trill, beating of wings in the trees
and the *vast rumble* of cars.
I am the one who sees, who listens.

Night or day, all is sight, life.

« *Une vache qui tousse dans la brume ...* »

Une vache qui tousse dans la brume, bruit effrayant.

Levé aujourd'hui à l'aurore.
Le battant blanc. La lueur sourde gagne une à une les poutres du plafond. Je me réveille tout à fait. L'étoffe blanche allumée sur le dossier. Le jour gagne les draps défaits. Encoignures. Je tire un peu le rideau : un grand coutelas livide refoule les nuages noirs et tassés, le ciel pavé de vagues,— naissance du bleu. Une fine lame de feu s'insère à l'extrémité entre la paroi des collines et le mur des nuages. Quelques taches noires comme de l'encre se détachent sur cette lamelle — arbres. La terre décolle. Changement d'aiguillage. L'heure où les sphères qui s'emboîtent se descellent. La ligne de suture est visible. La soudure. Heure éternellement brûlée par le sommeil, taie de l'homme.
J'ouvre la porte. Cette étrange lueur sourde, blancheur aveugle, sans éclat, gagne le pas de la porte. Il faut dire qu'il n'y a pas de cris. Je veux voir le point d'attache du soleil qui monte à droite de la maison.
Falaise — les larmes me viennent presque aux yeux devant cette petite valve de feu dépassant la terre qu'a dû si souvent voir Reverdy. « Le spectacle le plus émouvant qu'offre la Nature » — Règle de feu. Je marche droit dans la *tête sourde*. Marche à pas de loup. Peur d'être dévoré par les chiens. Mais je n'entends aucun aboiement. Le ciel est piqué de cris d'oiseaux invisibles. Cris des oiseaux dans *la rosée*. Espadrilles mouillées. Au retour, une vache tousse. Ce n'est pas la lumière de la réalité. Ce brasier dévore le ciel, sans crépiter. Il s'avance comme un planeur. On dirait qu'on est sorti de la terre. La terre somnambule. En raison de cet engourdissement total si bien perdu dans le jour brutal où j'écris maintenant. La lueur qui filtre à peine du sol, et les pierres blanches du chemin. On voyait un point lumineux, le roulement d'une voiture à l'autre bout du monde, à l'extrémité de la plaine. Quand la terre devient comme de la laine — dont quelques brins flambent. Peut-être devient-elle ainsi plus assimilable, colle-t-elle mieux à la tête. Quand il n'y a pas de mouches, pas de chaleur. Quand elle est sourde. Avant que la terre ne grésille. L'homme ôté. Qui à cette heure habituellement dort.
Trois nuages vaporeux flottaient au-dessus de la Seine, bien plus bas.   Je voulais mourir, avant de me lever. Je ne pouvais plus supporter l'idée de recommencer la journée. *Mais il faut vivre pour voir* l'aurore — la terre descellée.
Je me suis assis sur un rocher habituellement écrasé par le jour. Rocher trempé d'aurore. Maculé de ces taches de feu vif orange qui éclaboussent l'horizon. Lichen encore visible le jour, comme ces végétations marines, adhérant aux roches qui attendent l'heure de la marée pour s'épanouir. Un champ de nuages collait au même rocher, de disques noirs et blancs enchevêtrés, durement échoués comme ces tas de nuages pavés, durement tassés, écrasés les uns contre les autres, très bas. Le plafond bas du ciel. L'écorce du ciel qui se fendille.

'A cow that coughs in the fog...'

A cow that coughs in the fog, frightening noise.

Got up today at dawn.
The door panel, white. The dull glow reaches the beams along the ceiling one by one. I wake up completely. The white cloth, lit up on the backrest. Day reaches the rumpled sheets. Corners. I pull back the curtain a bit: a huge pale knife pushes back the black piled-up clouds, the sky paved with waves, — birth of blue. A thin blade of fire cuts into the edge between the partition of hills and the wall of clouds. A few black stains like ink stand out against this sliver — trees. The earth comes unstuck. Shifting of the rails. The hour when the spheres that interlock come loose. The suture is visible. The weld. Hour eternally burned by sleep, blind spot on the human eye.
I open the door. That strange dull glow, matte blind whiteness reaches the doorstep. It must be said there aren't any shouts. I want to see the sun's hinging point as it climbs to the right of the house.
Cliff — tears almost come to my eyes before this little valve of fire peeking over the earth that Reverdy must have seen so frequently. "The most moving spectacle offered by Nature" — Rule of fire. I walk straight on into the *muffled head*. Stealthily as a wolf. Fear of being eaten up by dogs. But I don't hear any barking. The sky is pricked by the calls of unseen birds. Calls of birds in *the dew*. Wet espadrilles. On the way back, a cow coughs. This isn't reality's light. This flame devours the sky, without crackling. It advances like a glider. You'd say we've left the earth. The sleepwalking earth. Because of this complete numbness so utterly lost in the brutal day during which I now write. The glow that scarcely filters from the ground, and the white stones of the path. You could see a shining point, a car rolling at the end of the earth, the far edge of the plain. When the earth becomes like wool — with several threads ablaze. Perhaps this is how it becomes easier to assimilate, cleaving better to the head. When there aren't any flies, any heat. When it is muffled. Before the earth sizzles. Man removed. Who at this hour is usually sleeping.
Three wispy clouds were floating over the Seine, much farther down.   I wanted to die, before getting up. I couldn't bear the idea of starting the day all over again. *But you have to live to see* the dawn — the earth unsealed.
I sat on a rock usually crushed by the light. Rock drenched with dawn. Stained by these smears of orange fire that spattered the horizon. Lichen still visible in the light, like those sea-plants, clinging to the rocks, that wait for the tide so they can bloom. A field of clouds stuck to the same rock, black and white discs entangled, harshly run aground like these piles of cobbled clouds, harshly packed together, crushed against each other, very low. The low ceiling of the sky. The sky's bark that splits.

Le rocher brillait extraordinairement. Comme un bloc de ciel. Criblé de lichen orange. Dans le village, au départ. *Pierraille*
pan de pierres écroulées. Mur dur sourd aveugle au-dessous du bol de feu, muet, de la grande tasse d'eau de l'aube.
Le soc rougi qui laboure la terre.
Lumière aigre de la première lampe au fond du village
au centre des toits.

The rock glittered astoundingly. Like a block of sky. Riddled with orange
lichen. In the village, at the outset. *Reverdy's stones*
rock-face collapsed. Hard blind deaf wall below the bowl of fire, mute, below
dawn's great cup of water.
The reddened plowshare that tills the earth.
Sharp light of the first lamp deep within the village
                              in the middle of the rooftops.

« La ville, le champ, brûle sans bruit... »

La ville, le champ, brûle sans bruit.

Après tous ces textes de l'œil fermé

IL FAUT PASSER AU-DEHORS

                                    la terre au pas de course
dans les massacres
                        nous qui devons voir les choses de si loin
                    nous qui sommes entourés de murs et de champs
c'est toujours la nouvelle qui circule
on n'y croira pas avant d'être déchiqueté
que les murs, le ciel pavé de vagues, les mouches bourdonnent
au plafond

car on a laissé passer trop de temps. En une seule nuit, trop de
temps s'est écoulé. Il n'est presque plus temps. On ne *voit* plus
rien (dans les champs, la lumière, les mouches bourdonnantes,
qui tournent). Il faut brûler les étapes. Marche forcée de la vue.
                    pour entendre ces terribles cris d'enfants

'The city, the field, burning soundless...'

The city, the field, burning soundless.

After all these texts with closed eyes

WE HAVE TO GO OUTSIDE

                              earth on the run
in massacres
                  we who must see things from so faraway
                   who're surrounded by walls and fields
there's always news that gets around
we don't believe it till we're ripped apart
that the walls, the sky cobbled with waves, the flies buzz
on the ceiling

time has elapsed. There's no more time, almost. We don't
see anything anymore (in the fields, the light, the buzzing
flies that swirl). We must move at breakneck speed. Forced
march of sight.
                 to hear these children's terrible cries

« Aube sans soleil... »

Aube sans soleil
d'emblée blanche.

De la falaise : une immense foulée de nuages suspendue au dessus du cours de la Seine. Cette chaîne blanche s'entre-ouvre au-dessus de l'île comme l'œil d'une aiguille.

Champs magiques, comme une plage de sèches et de goémon, fraîchement abandonnés par la mer. Couleurs encore réservées — arêtes aiguës, dentelle des chardons clairs comme des vitres — éveil des points jaunes et violets avant de s'être remués.

À l'aube : tout ce qui est usé devient neuf et usé. Des objets usés — flambant neufs — pas encore fatigués par le jour — comme les pierres du chemin qui rayonnent.
Voilà la source éternelle qui nous est infusée pendant notre sommeil — que l'on peut surprendre si on est réveillé vers la fin de la nuit : on s'arrache à vue d'œil des vapeurs de la nuit.
Le corps de vapeur s'étend sous les pieds *comme une foulée de nuages*. Le soleil monte dans la poitrine avant même d'apparaître à l'horizon de la chambre, entre les croisées noires et le monticule noir qui se détache sur le jour, l'aube nous laboure.

La tête jaillit dans son champ, les amarres soudain coupées
— pour un peu, on chanterait comme les coqs.

'Dawn without sun...'

Dawn without sun
white straightaway.

From the cliff: an immense trampling of clouds suspended above the flow of the Seine. This white chain cracks open above the island like a needle's eye.

Magical fields, like a beach of cuttlefish and kelp newly abandoned by the sea. Colors still preserved — sharp fishbones, lace of thistles bright as window-panes — awakening of yellow and purple dots before they've stirred.

At dawn: everything that's worn becomes both new and worn. Worn objects — brand-new — not yet tired out by day — like the stones of the path that glow.
Here is the unending spring we're steeped in as we sleep — that we can glimpse when we're awakened toward the end of night: we catch sight of night's mists.
The body of mist spreads underfoot *like the trampling of clouds*. The sun rises in our chest even before it appears on the room's horizon; between the black casements, the black knoll standing out against the light, dawn plows us.

The head shoots up in its field, its tethers suddenly cut
— it wouldn't take much for us to crow like roosters.

« La buée étouffe doucement la vue »

La buée étouffe doucement la vue
        limitée aux cercles bien distincts des arbustes
        et du chemin qui tinte.
        À partir de l'épaule, la terre s'incline sur le sentier et
roule en poudre dans l'air au-dessous du pan d'herbes
                au-dessus des touffes —

le ciel hermétiquement blanc au-dessous.
              au-dessus —
entre deux valves — on adhère encore —

L'herbe, que les vaches broutent, est molle et tendre, comme
de l'algue.

'Mist gently smothers sight…'

Mist gently smothers sight
        reduced to the clear-cut circles of the bushes
        and the path that hums.
        Starting from the shoulder, the earth slopes on the trail and
rolls as powder through the air under the grass patch
                above the tufts —

the sky hermetically white below.
                      above —
between two valves — we still cling —

The grass where the cows graze is tender and soft, like
seaweed.

« *Et je puis dire que mon orgueil...* »

et je puis dire que mon orgueil n'est pas véhément,
est aussi faible que celui de la terre
il rayonne faiblement

je ne suis qu'un reflet
et la bouche même de la nature
je ne me reconnais pas
je ne m'appartiens pas
pas plus que le jour ne m'appartient
je me trouverais devant moi que je ne me reconnaîtrais pas
       n'étant que l'instrument sans nom de cette vérité
       qui se trouve en dehors de moi

mon travail —

       je me risque à être sur terre
je me risque à poser ma main sur le jour

'And I can say that my pride...'

and I can say that my pride isn't strident,
is feeble as that of the earth
it feebly shines

I'm only a reflection
and the very mouth of nature
I don't recognize myself
I don't belong to myself
any more than daylight belongs to me
facing myself, I wouldn't recognize myself
   since I'm only the nameless instrument of this truth
   which lies outside me

my work —

    I venture to be on earth
I venture to lay my hand on the light

Fragments de cahier, 1952-1954

ma fille — tu ne la reconnaîtras pas.
tu diras — voila de l'air
une colline — une fin de journée
que chantent des oiseaux —
tout ce qui est impalpable, reconnaissable
— et ce sera ma fille
apparue dans un poème

mon poème court sans cesse
en avant de moi
comme si à l'extrémité l'air
avait pris feu

je raye le jour, comme
un éclat de verre
ou de voix

ce que la poésie dessèche n'a pas besoin d'eau   ce qu'elle assèche

éclaire
eau moins rapide que les pierres

Notebook fragments, 1952–1954

my daughter — you will not recognize her.
you'll say — there's air
a hill — birds singing
the end of a day —
all that's impalpable, recognizable
and that will be my daughter
appearing in a poem

my poem runs ceaselessly
in front of me
            as if the edge of the air
                had caught fire

I scratch out the day, like
a shard of glass
                or voice

what poetry withers needs no water   what it dries

                                            sheds light
                water slower than stones

En aval

L'enfant cogne. La boule dure de la tête file comme une anguille. Tout le monde est fardé de lumière. Le store. Mêlée de chaises et de meubles blonds accrochés aux battants. L'ombre portée de l'arbre plonge dans la nuit de la vitre supportée par un grand T blanc. Un peu plus haut, juste au-dessous du ciel, miroitent les lucarnes des glaciers.

Downstream

The child knocks. The hard ball of the head wriggles like an eel. The whole world is rouged with light. The blinds. Jumble of chairs and blond furniture hanging from the windows. The shadow cast by the tree plunges into the night of the windowpane held up by a large white T. A little higher, just below the sky, the glaciers' skylights shimmer.

La terre

La porte décousue, couchée en travers. Le mufle de l'herbe, comme un morceau de sucre, tout à la furie des insectes, au bas du parapet où elle souffle.

The earth

The door disjointed, lying on its side. The nose of the grass, like a lump of sugar, assailed by the insects, at the base of the wall where it breathes.

Vu

La mer entre par la porte ouverte et se
promène sur le seuil. À gauche souffle de la
poussière en petits tourbillons. Une lampe-
tempete oscille auprès d'un grand feu.

Seen

The sea enters through the open door and strolls on the threshold. Blows some dust to the left in small whirlwinds. A storm lamp swings beside a big fire.

Varengeville

Aucune fable dont farder ou accuser le profile de
ces collines de cette nuit pour rétablir la continuité
rompue de la lune échevelée vue par l'échancrure de
la falaise à la lune ronde de l'herbe chaude et rase
du plateau
la falaise s'éboule l'air reste ouvert
le mouvement de la marée déplace les tribus de poissons
jusqu'à ce qu'ils donnent du museau dans la vitrine
migration de toutes les bêtes (à valves, à coquilles,
à pattes)
relève des algues
les nuages vapeurs à des hauteurs filent obstinément
dans un sens indécis
deux bateaux illuminés se croisent en pleine mer
sous l'œil des phares
un homme
il a tout le temps de se perdre, dans cet espace ni
amical ni hostile mais dépourvu de signification
mythique
(il n'en sait rien ; il voudrait bien ; sur lui descend
une nuit froide, muette, bizarre, qui le tourmente
en le pénétrant de son infériorité par rapport à une
autre époque : enfantillage des approches de minuit.
Éboulis de craie vétuste et de silex à déblayer sur le
sentier abrupt.)

Varengeville

No tale is needed to disguise or reveal the profile of
these hills on this night to restore the broken line from the
disheveled moon seen through the fissure in the cliff to the
round moon of the warm short grass on
the plateau
the cliff collapses the air remains open
the movement of the tide shifts the swarms of fish
until they bump their muzzles on the window case
migration of all creatures (shellfish, bivalves,
with legs)
seaweed takes its turn
high up the hazy clouds stubbornly steam by
in an uncertain direction
two illumined boats cross on the open sea
under the lighthouses' gaze
a man
he has all the time to lose himself in this space that's
neither friendly nor hostile but devoid of mythical
meaning
(he knows nothing about this; he'd like to; a cold night
descends on him, mute, strange, that torments him with
a piercing sense of his own inferiority to another era:
childishness of midnight's vicinity. Scree of worn-down
chalk and flint to clear from the steep trail.)

La préhistoire

Dans cet entre deux mondes détestable
avant l'avènement de la morale
la mémoire mercenaire
que le soleil frappe

en pleine craie.

Prehistory

In this hateful gap between two worlds
before morality's advent
mercenary memory
which the sun strikes

right out of limestone.

Points de chute

    Les contreforts gonflés comme
des voiles, les crêtes noires qui
s'abattent le long du papier, or des
paroles, suivant la ligne, pillant
la houle.

Drop-off points

The abutments swollen like sails,
the black crests that collapse along
the paper, gold of words, following
the line, pillaging
the swell.

Élargissement

Que la lumière l'éclaire jusqu'au fond, recule ses murs blancs et la couvre d'un plafond.   La chambre.   L'œil calme du papier. La porte sèche.

Le revers du feu brûle dans la chambre. Air lisse, sans un nœud. Glacé à l'endroit.

Lit calé dans le mur d'angle.   Jour équarri.

Fenêtre de la personne sur la fraîcheur sans qu'elle penche.

Dans l'autre pièce, les volets deviennent blancs.

Un bras tendu à deux étages de la terre, dans le souffle.

Enlargement

Let the light illumine it all the way, push its white walls back
and cover it with a ceiling.   The room.   The paper's calm eye.
The dry door.

Fire's other side burns in the room. Smooth air, without a knot.
Freezing from the inside out.

Bed wedged at an angle into the wall.   Daylight squared-off.

Someone's window onto coolness without leaning out.

In the other room, the shutters turn white.

An arm held out two floors from earth, into breath.

Nature sèche

Traduire l'ornière, oscillant dans le sillage tendre de l'or clair du couvercle que je cloue.

Terre de gorge.

Il y a un bras recruté dans le caillou, une roue dans cette brosse, un grain serré dans le ruban de paille qui a roulé dans les narines du chemin. Des animaux se heurtent à la clôture. Les pierres détachées de leur ombre s'arrêtent au fond.

Je sors dans l'air pour la dernière fois.

Je vois tout un quartier du ciel accroché loin du clou.

Un coq éclate.

J'attends, la tête à moitié fermée, la monnaie de feu qui tachera le mur. Le piéton tranquille qui avance, un pain à la main, dans le vent. La route le porte en avant, jusqu'à ce ciel qui roule son grain. Le camion de grain s'enfonce lourdement.

Dry life

Translating the rut, back and forth in the tender wash of the light
gold cover I'm nailing.

Throated soil.

There's an arm growing back in the stone, a wheel in this brush,
a seed packed in the ribbon of straw that rolled in the nostrils of the
path. Animals bump up against the fence. The stones
loosed from their shadow halt at the end.

I go out into the air for the last time.

I see an entire swath of sky hung far from the nail.

A rooster bursts out.

I await, my head half closed, the coin of fire that will mark
the wall. A quiet walker, bread in hand, moves in the wind.
The road carries him forward, all the way to this sky that
trundles its grain. The grain truck slowly bogs down.

Autre ressort

Ce texte comme une pierre perdue, une deuxième fois arraché à la terre, dans la chambre qui m'enrobe. Exposé au feu insignifiant, au feu imaginaire. Tu n'opposes rien à la nuit, au jour agrandi. Inséparable de ce qui est ouvert, de la lumière ambulante.

J'ai négligé l'air blanc qui s'abat autour de nous sans un mot, jusqu'à la pluie sans reproche, au cri des moellons.

Retenus par la pierre, le plâtre immédiat, à l'abri de la chambre
ou du rocher.

Pour suivre la trace du vent, jusqu'au feu glacé, à l'endroit où se
tenait l'arbre, la terre inoccupée, où tu te tenais.
Du plateau au feu limpide à l'air desséché de la route à laquelle nous
sommes adossés.
Vent, mais feu, vraiment, jusqu'au talon, au jour noir, au bord du
front.
Le vent souffle comme en pleine nuit.

La partie blanche et la partie
bruyante

j'ai reconnu le jour exact

dans sa nudité

qui s'éclaircit
et se glace

son exacte nudité

la paroi sans tableau
les ardoises

les glaciers

la neige des vitres des
glaciers.

Another recourse

This text like a lost stone, torn from the earth a second time, in the room that cloaks me. Exposed to the meaningless fire, the imaginary fire. You do nothing to counter the night, the widened day. Indivisible from what is open, from the wandering light.
I neglected the white air that pours down around us without a word, up until the blameless rain, the rubble's shout.

Held back by the stone and the plaster nearer by, in the shelter of the room or the rock.

In order to follow the wind's track, to the freezing fire, to the place where the tree stood, the unoccupied land, where you stood as well.
From the plateau's crystal fire to the parched air of the road we lean against.
Wind, but truly fire, all the way to the heel, to the black day, to the forehead's edge.
The wind blows as in the thick of night.

What is white and what makes
noise

I recognized the exact day

in its nakedness

which lights up
and freezes

its exact nakedness

the pictureless wall
the slate slabs

the glaciers

the snow of the glaciers'
glass panes.

Cette chambre dont je vois déjà les gravats, comme une montagne blanche qui nous chasse de l'endroit où nous dormons.

La montagne qui nous chasse, le pain sans répit.

This room I already see as rubble, like a white mountain that drives us out of the place where we sleep.

The mountain that drives us out, the bread without reprieve.

Le voyage

Rien ne distingue la route des accidents de ce ciel.
Nous allons sur la paille molle et froide de ce ciel, — à peine plus
froide que nous, par grandes brassées, comme un feu rompu dont il faut
franchir le genou, qui s'éclipse.
Je tiens deux mains chaudes, deux mains de paille. Un front paille
avance près de moi dans le champ obscur, sous ce genou blanc. Entre
mes membres et ma voix, — le sol, avant le matin.

L'horizon est proche du seuil de la pièce où je suis perdu.

L'arbre ou la carrosserie qui recueille un moment l'horizon.

Le ciel est plus accessible que la terre sur laquelle nous marchons.
Mais je n'ai pas surpris la terre ou le ciel en me levant, en descendant
dans l'air.
Le champ plat.
Le champ où j'ai frappé, que je repousse jusqu'à l'arbre. Cette terre
qui sort de la terre et qui ne bouge pas. J'entends le vent.

Par la fenêtre ouverte qui donne sur une porte ouverte, je vois le mur
de la rue.

À l'aube j'ai été surpris de ne pas pouvoir éteindre.
Je serai aussi bien expliqué que le buisson, — encore là. Deux doigts
froids, deux pincées de terre aux coins des yeux. À nos doigts se mêle la tête
sèche de l'herbe. J'ai toujours cette demeure de brume au coin du visage.
Aux premières lueurs du jour.

Remercié d'un plaisir que je ne donne pas.

The journey

Nothing divides the road from the accidents of this sky.
We walk on the soft, cold straw of this sky — hardly colder than ourselves —
in great armfuls, like a dying fire whose lap we have to cross
as it fades away.

I'm holding two warm hands, two hands of straw. A straw forehead
moves beside me in the dark field, under this white lap. Between my limbs
and my voice — the ground, before morning.

The horizon nears the threshold of the room where I'm lost.

The tree, or bodywork, collects the horizon for a while.

The sky is more accessible than the earth on which we walk.
But I have not startled the earth or sky by rising, by descending
in the air.

The flat field.

The field I've struck, pushing it back to the tree. This earth that
comes out of earth and does not budge. I hear the wind.

Through the window open on an open door, I see the wall of the
street.

At dawn, I was surprised I couldn't turn it off.

I'll be as well explained as the bush—still there. Two cold fingers,
two pinches of earth at the corners of the eyes. The dry head of the grass
mingles with our fingers. Fog always dwells at the corner of my face.

At the first gleams of day.

Thanked for a pleasure I don't give.

Le lent travail du métal des faux à travers les pierres. La terre houleuse fulmine.

Une nouvelle clarté, plus forte, nous prend les mains. L'espace qui est entre nous s'agrandit comme si le ciel, où le double visage s'embue, reculait démesurément.

Je vis de ce que l'air délaisse et dont je démêle à peine ce regard qui finit de s'épuiser dans la terre froide au goût de brûlé.

<blockquote>

Ici
et rien

cette route

la dérision
des murs
l'épaule froide

les draps
le vent se lève.

</blockquote>

La lumière ne contamine pas le jour. L'eau ne la fait pas siffler.

Je regarde l'air animé comme si, avant l'horizon lisse, j'étais embarrassé du corps que j'embrasse. Sur ce sol encore retourné, — où le jour en suspens vient s'abreuver à mon pied, comme fixé dans sa blanche indécision. Comme un arbre.

Comme la veste de ce glacier que l'usure couvre de son givre.

Mon arrivée, ma sortie de terre. Je reviens du fin fond des terres à ces confins, — à l'heure où le jour brûle encore sur les bords, ou y fait courir un cordon de feu. Mais la paroi blanche, — dorée, glacée par la lumière qui la rehausse et y fait courir de faibles montagnes.

L'air dans lequel je me dissipe.

The metal of the scythes, their slow work through the stones. The heaving earth seethes.

A new, stronger clarity takes us by the hand. The space between us grows as if the sky, where the double face mists over, were endlessly pulling back.

I live on what the air gives up, from which I barely tease this gaze that ends up dwindling into the chill, burnt-tasting earth.

Here
and nothing

this road

the mockery
of walls
the cold shoulder

the sheets
the rising wind.

The light doesn't taint the day. The water doesn't make it ring.

I watch the lively air as if, before the smooth horizon, I were embarrassed by the body I embrace. On this still-tilled ground — where the unsettled day comes to drink at my feet, as though intent on its blank indecision. Like a tree.

Like the jacket of this glacier, covered by the frost of wear and tear.

My arrival, my exit from earth. I return from the farthest reaches of the land to this frontier — at the hour when day still smolders at the edges, or girds it with a cordon of fire. But the white cliff-face—gilded and glazed by the light that picks it out and sweeps it with dim mountains.

The air into which I dissolve.

Même lorsque le cadre terrestre est dans le feu, que l'évidence se dissipe sur ce dos excorié, comme le pas sur le cadre des routes, — plus qu'il ne fuit.

Il n'y a pas de route, mais le jour élargi qui me laisse aux prises avec ce sol où il s'incruste. Au moment où la terre se cristallise, se raréfie, — et, avant le dernier bond, fait demi-tour, disparaît.

Comme le champ qui afflue jusqu'à la clôture grande ouverte où il s'arrête, pendant que le soleil, à la fin du jour, nous inonde de sa glace, et disparaît.

Mais toujours, dans l'air cristallin, le front têtu de la clôture qui, si possible, se fait plus proche, — bien que nos pieds soient libérés de la poussière qui anéantit comme du sol froid. Je sais encore, sur ce foyer piétiné et froid qui se sépare lentement de son feu, que derrière moi l'oreille brûlante du soleil me suit, — sans même relever la tête vers le champ rose, avant que la nuit roule et nous ait anéantis.

Comme une goutte d'eau en suspens, — avant que la terre se dilue. Je vois la terre aride.

Devant cette paroi qui s'ouvre, front traversé par le vent qui devance le visage et s'approfondit, un arbre comme un mur sans fenêtre, — à côté du ciel révélé au tournant de la route basse et froide qu'il regagne, comme une porte toujours ouverte.

Elle —, l'éclat, la tête impérieuse du jour.

À l'instant où le feu communiqué à l'air s'efface, où la blancheur du jour gagne, — sans soleil. La terre de ce champ pauvre dont nous sépare le talus du jour.

Cheminant vers le blanc mur bleu devant lequel j'ai toujours fait demi-tour, j'avance lentement dans l'air pour atteindre à l'immobilité de l'autre mur.

Au moment de cette fracture, du silence subit, où l'air affligé d'un dernier remous se stabilise et dure.

L'air qui s'empare des lointains nous laisse vivants derrière lui.

Even when the frame of earth is dipped in fire, let simple clarity melt away on this scar-riddled back, like our footsteps on the frame of the roads — rather than flee.

There is no road, only the widened day that leaves me grappling with the ground where it's encrusted. At the moment when earth crystallizes, rarefied — and before the last leap, wheels around and disappears.
Like the field that flows toward the wide-open fence where it stops, while the sun, at the end of day, floods us with its ice, and disappears.
But all this time, in the crystalline air, the stubborn forehead of the fence, if possible, draws nearer — even if our feet are freed from the dust that razes us like cold ground. I still know, on this cold, trampled hearth that slowly parts from its fire, that the sun's burning ear trails behind me—without even raising my head toward the rosy field, before night rolls and has razed us.

Like a suspended drop of water — before the earth is diluted. I see the arid earth.

Before this cliff-face that opens, forehead traversed by the wind that outstrips the face and goes deep, a tree like a windowless wall — beside the sky revealed at the bend of the cold, low road which it rejoins, like a still-open door.
Door — the resplendence, the commanding head of day.
At the moment when the fire suffusing air fades away, when the whiteness of day prevails — without sun. Slope of day that divides us from this meager field of earth.

Walking toward the blank blue wall where I've always turned back, I slowly move into the air to reach the standstill of the other wall.
At the moment of this breakage, a sudden silence when the air, troubled by a final swirl, steadies and holds.

The air, engulfing distances, leaves us alive in its wake.

Avant que la blancheur

Avant que la blancheur du soleil soit aussi
proche que ta main, j'ai couru sans m'éteindre.

Dans l'obscurité du jour, tout n'est, sur cette
route, que chute,
            et éclats. Jusqu'à ce que le soir
ait fusé.

Notre route n'est pas rompue par la chaleur qui
nous renvoie,
        éclairés. Sans que tu t'arrêtes à
cette chaleur. La route où je sombre encore me
devance, comme le vent.

J'ignore la route sur laquelle notre souffle se
retire. Le jour, en tombant, m'entoure.

Ma main, reprise déjà, fend à peine la sécheresse,
            le flamboiement.

Before the whiteness

Before the sun's whiteness came close as your
hand, I ran without burning out.

In the day's darkness, everything on this road
falls
          and splinters. Until the evening bursts
forth.

Our road isn't broken by the heat that sends
us back,
          illumined. Without the heat stopping you.
The road where I'm sinking still forestalls me,
like the wind.

I don't know on what road our breath withdraws.
The day, setting, surrounds me.

My hand, already taken back, barely splits the drought,
          the blazing.

Solstice

                                Puisqu'au-dessous du vent,
nous nous sommes arrêtés, où, après le soleil, tu ne l'attendais pas,
j'ai franchi, l'été, comme une masse éclatée, la montagne,
                                                lié les deux
                        soleils.

        La chaleur bientôt.

Solstice

                                        Since we stopped
under the wind where, after the sun, you weren't expecting it,
I crossed the mountain in summer, like a mass blown apart,
                                        I bound the two
                suns together.

    Soon the heat.

La terre...

                                              La terre,
et en avant, aussi aveugle que soleil après la retombée.

                              Pour te rejoindre je reviens.

The earth...

The earth,

and onward, as blind as sun after the fallout.

To catch up with you I come back.

Avant le matin

        Tout l'air du dehors imprègne la pièce.
Le jour le projette contre cette blanche paroi.

      Pas plus que le brasier blanc du matin, comme on approche
               de la lumière,
                    du froid. Comme la poitrine
ouverte, du matin froid.

     L'air lisse

     le sol et l'air

     la terre comme une pièce
     dans l'intervalle du feu.

     Le jour
     avec les travaux du jour
     le blanc des murs

     je me range
     avant de prendre feu
     comme le vent

     au début du matin.

Before morning

All the air from outside soaks the room.
The day casts it on this white wall.

Nothing but morning's white blaze, as we draw near
the light,
the cold. Like an opened
chest, toward the cold morning.

Smooth air

ground and air

the earth as a room
amid the fire.

The day
with the day's work
the white of the walls

I settle down
before catching fire
like the wind

at morning's start.

Porteur d'un livre dans la montagne

... chute de neige, vers la fin du jour, de plus en plus épaisse, dans laquelle vient s'immobiliser un *convoi sans destination — je tiens le jour...* La paupière du nuage porteur de la neige se levant, je me retrouve inclus dans le bleu de l'autre jour.

Son pourtour semblable aux montants mal ajustés d'un cadre métallique mobile, je l'avais cependant — sans aucune application possible — solidement tenu entre mes mains, déjà chemin ferré étréci sur l'enclume de l'un des forgerons ayant donné de loin en loin, autrefois, dans la vallée, le timbre de lieux habités aujourd'hui déserts. Hier encore, nous en parlions. La brusquerie du froid qui s'était abattu, par la suite, avec l'orage, n'est plus, entre mes draps, qu'un souvenir dont je démêle mal, en plein été, s'il provient d'un livre ou d'un village. Le froid, soudainement avivé par la sonnerie inattendue de l'orage, et auquel, toute trace de chaleur disparue, s'ajoutait alors celui de la nuit, se déposait en neige dans ma tête, bloquant les voies...

Bearer of a book in the mountains

... snowfall, towards the end of day, thicker and thicker, in which a *train without destination* comes to a standstill — *I hold the day* ... As the eyelid of the cloud bearing the snow is raised, I find myself included in the other day's blue.

Its rim, similar to the badly adjusted mounts of a moving metal frame, I had nonetheless — without any possible purpose — already held in my hands, solidly: already an iron-clad path, honed on the anvil of one of the blacksmiths, used to give you in the valley, as you approached long ago, the note of inhabited places now deserted. Only yesterday, we were talking about it. The abruptness of the cold that afterwards descended with the storm, is no more, between my sheets, than a memory I can hardly figure out in the midst of summer, whether it comes from a book or from a village. The cold, suddenly ringing with the storm's unexpected alarm, which the night-chill had deepened, erasing any trace of heat, was settling like snow in my head, blocking the rails ...

Un village ou un livre, les lignes
étrécies étant celles d'une tranche — au possible — jusqu'à ces lèvres …

Enclume de fraîcheur, comme je le tiens je n'en serai plus délogé.

… parole — non cela, la parole, elle seule, le dit, scindant.

Le convoi est bloqué. Pas de destination, étant là — dans la consistance de
cette neige…

… après soi comme inclus dans la langue — le jour.

… pas de destination : j'ai rejoint.
Mais la parole qui le rapporte, je dois encore aller jusqu'à elle : comme à pied.
Une glose obscurcit ou éclaire.

A village or a book, the narrowed
lines being those of cars connected — as much as possible — up to these lips…

Anvil of coolness: since I hold it, I will not be driven out.

… word — no : that is said by the word alone, a splitting-apart.

The train is blocked. No destination, being there — in the consistency of
this snow…

… after yourself as included in the language — day.

… no destination : I've caught up.
But the word that brings it back, I must still go up to that word : as if
on foot. A gloss darkens or sheds light.

Lettre

... écrit à la clarté des eaux sèches.

... et dans la page

que sur soi on a tournée en avançant.

... le bleu qui subjugue.

... avoir fendu le bleu indifférent à la soif.

... à-plat du vent

conforme à l'autre tête couvrant.

... aveuglement fendu, si je rejoins demain.   comme le bleu
indifférent à la soif.

... sans toi, ce que je suis :   pur chemin.

Letter

. . . written in the light of dry waters.

. . . and in the page

moving forward we have turned on ourselves.

. . . the blue that subdues.

. . . to have split the blue indifferent to thirst.

. . . the wind's down-flat

matching another head that covers.

. . . blindness split, if I rejoin tomorrow.   like the blue
indifferent to thirst.

. . . without you, what I am: path, and path only.

Eau, en arménien, se dit *djour*.
Village: *ghyour*.

(O. Mandelstam)

village et eau.   et eau, de glacier.

djour — dans la langue soudain, et par ce surcroît de l'éloignement, que moi-même j'aurai ignorée, que j'ignore toujours, et une fois pour toutes vraisemblable- ment — de l'eau.   là, j'entends —   un tel mot, avant même de prendre sur moi de le prononcer — *déjà*. *dès aujourd'hui*, dans ma langue qui, du coup, elle, sera l'étrangère aussi.

Notes on translation

Water, in Armenian, is called *djour*.
Town: *ghyour*.

(O. Mandelstam)

town and water.   and water, glacial.

djour   —   suddenly in the language, and by this
surplus of distance that I ignored, that I always ignore,
seemingly once and for all   —   water.   there, I
hear — such a word, even before taking it upon my-
self to pronounce it   —   *already. from now on*, in
my language that will become, for that reason, foreign
as well.

l'eau, se boit.   le village :   il se prononcera.   ni village
ni eau quelquefois : mais empilement de lauzes dépareillées
analogues par endroits à des assiettes dans la sécheresse.

                                                        village.
                        glacier.   l'eau ira de glacier
à village.   retourne, de même que la parole
sur sa soif qui assèche, et comme le courant noue, du village
au glacier.

carton glacé — ou carte — glissé — placé — entre
les feuillets, est-ce là que, voulant suspendre la lecture
brusquement désordonnée, au passage j'ai pu traduire par
glacier.

j'ai — pour atteindre plus vite au dehors, traduit par glacier.
. . . .

traduire, je ne peux pas : je serai traduit — alors même
qu'à cela j'ai voulu m'appliquer.
. . . .

the water, drinks itself. the town: will utter itself. neither
town nor water sometimes but stacks of mismatched slate
arranged like folds of stone in the drought.

                                                                town.
            glacier.   the water will go from glacier
to town.   returns, the same as speech
on drying thirst, and as the current loops, from the town to
the glacier.

glossy cardboard — or card — slid — placed — between
the pages, it's there that, wanting to suspend my reading,
abruptly disordered, in passing I could translate by
glacier.

I   —   to get outside faster, translated by glacier.
.   .   .   .

translate: I cannot: I will be translated — even if that's
what I strove to do.
.   .   .   .

dans le sol de la pièce, trouver — et premier à être parti, le
toit. sous les pieds, un sol de nouveau — et, comme on ira
   rouvert.

qui aura dressé les murs, lui-même — comme aujourd'hui
par-dessus ma tête, le jour — est passé par une épaisseur
de terre.

                        gagner,
comme on s'y heurte, l'ouvert pareil à un morceau de jour.

               le mot — aujourd'hui un mot,
il a fallu que je revienne l'habiter.

eau n'était pas dans la langue.   *village* n'était pas
dans la langue.

. . . .

l'autre jour, le fumiste : à entendre les mots de la langue qui
a fini de se perdre par ici, il était certain, enfant, que ces mots
pour lui sans obscurité, la grand-mère chaque jour les inven-
tait à son intention.

find, in the floor of the room   —   the first to go, the
roof. underfoot, another ground   —   and, as we'll go
    reopened.

he who erected the walls, himself   —   like the day
over my head today   —   passed through a thickness
of earth.

                                                            reach,
as we bump against it, the opening, like a piece of day.

                                    the word   —   today a word,
I had to come back and inhabit it.

water wasn't in the language.   *town* wasn't
in the language.
    .   .   .   .

the other day, the idler: to hear the words of the language
that was no longer lost here, he was sure, as a child, that
these words he saw in utter clarity, his grandmother in-
vented them each day especially for him.

expatrier.   rapatrier.

papier, par le travers de la parole qu'il aura supportée.
comme la plaque de neige couvrant.

. . . .

                      j'ai traduit —
pour l'y avoir placé à nouveau, ce qui était hors du livre
et n'est pas un mot.

nous nous y retrouverons.

en plusieurs langues , nous nous retrouverons.

. . . .

peut-être, par le travers de la parole, elles aussi les choses
auront-elles pu voir.

. . . .

dans *coché*, entendre : *écorché*   oui,
                   j'avais bien entendu.

expatriate.   repatriate.

paper, through the words it will hold up,
like the covering patch of snow.
. . . .

                             I translated —
to put down again, what was outside the book
and isn't a word.

there we'll find ourselves again.

in many languages, we'll find ourselves.
. . . .

perhaps, through speech, things too can
see.
. . . .
. . .

in *scraped*, hear: *skinned*   yes,
                  I'd heard clearly.

neige.   glace.   eau.   si vous êtes des mots, parlez.

                                  de nouveau,
l'injonction de l'enfant, cassante.

                                    l'inhumain.
la fraîche inhumanité. il y faut deux langues, au moins. deux
fois la langue, comme je passerai.   retenir quelque chose
du seuil de l'inhabité dans la langue quand on y sera entré.

la fraîcheur de l'inhumain, comme le vent.   d'un mot à un
autre, comme le vent.

. . . .
. . . .

snow.   ice.   water.   if you are words, speak.

                        again,
the child's order, sharp.

                          the inhuman.
the fresh inhumanity. it needs two languages, at least. twice
the language, as I'll pass.   keep something of the
uninhabited threshold in the language once you've entered in.

the freshness of the inhuman, like the wind.   from one word
to another, like the wind.

. . . .
. . . .

                                        pour
entendre, avant d'avoir parlé.

le natal.   non, je ne nommerai pas qui, dans les montagnes,
se sera en pleine nuit allongé sur la route, appliquant l'oreille
contre l'empierrement, pour tenter alors   —   il y a un siècle
et quelque   —   près de deux siècles   —   de percevoir le
roulement de la roue du courrier porteur de nouvelles, on ne
sait plus lesquelles, attendues, et, son espoir ne s'étant pas
matérialisé, comme à côté de soi a pu, se remettant debout,
aviser tout d'un coup les étoiles   —   leur éclat, dans sa
férocité   —   telles que jamais encore il ne les avait perçues.

                        moments, ici, où la terre se sera étoilée,
montagnes.
. . . .
. . . .

                                        aujourd'hui,
comme jour de toutes les routes perdues — mais le jour.

to

hear, before speaking.

the place of birth.   no, I won't name who, in the mountains,
will in the dead of night lie down on the road, pressing his ear
against the pavement, in order to try to   — a century ago
and more   — nearly two centuries   — perceive the
rolling of the courier's wheel, bringing awaited news, lost to
time, and, his hope not yet materialized, as he stands once
more, he suddenly glimpses the stars close by   — their
shining, in its ferocity   — as he's never seen them before.

moments, here, when the earth will be starry,
mountains.
. . . .
. . . .

today,

like day from all the lost roads   — but the day.

traduire, je ne peux pas.

sur l'occurrence d'un mot qui, dans l'autre langue — c'est
la mienne — sera perdu, faire halte à nouveau.

montagnes — ici, où l'on ne parle que rarement, pour la
langue je viens ici.

l'air — une poignée de main.

le reste,
avec les mots, s'étant momentanément retiré, les montagnes
demeureront seules, un moment.

rugueux, le vide : il préfigure — de même que, sous les yeux
pourtant, ce que je ne vois pas encore.   ce que, sans avoir
saisi non plus, dans le fond de la gorge,   sur la crête des
diphtongues, par des voyelles ouvertes là aussi,   je peux
entendre.

translate, I cannot.

upon the occurrence of a word that, in the other language —
which is mine — will be lost, halt once more.

mountains — here, where speaking is rare, for the language
I come here.

the air   —   a handshake.

the rest,
with the words, having momentarily withdrawn, the mountains
will stay alone, for a moment.

rugged, the emptiness: it prefigures — same as, even though
it's before my eyes, what I don't yet see. what without having
grasped it either, in the gorge of the throat,   on the crest
of the diphthongs, through the vowels open there too,   I can
hear.

la langue étrangère,
c'est la langue étrangère dans la langue.

morceau d'espace revenu balbutier au bord de l'espace.

sur un retrait
des langues, aujourd'hui, on avancera, par instants privé de
la langue.

le mot
sorti des mots, comme il a touché aux choses, enjoint : parlez.

oui, à côté, de nouveau.
de ce qui à l'instant m'a traversé l'esprit.

« alors, tu seras l'imbécile de ta pensée. »

l'espace. un morceau d'espace, séparé — comme d'un mot
à un autre, lorsqu'ensemble l'un et l'autre ils seront traversés
— de la séparation.

le morcellement, je respire, il disparaît, c'est l'espace.

un morceau d'espace.
cela peut être le nuage anachronique, une chute, un glaçon,
de l'eau avalée quand on a soif, le mur encore, ou
l'empierrement de la route à l'aplomb comme à soi elle sera
venue brusquement, instant de tout ce qui sépare...

. . . .

the foreign language
is the language foreign within the language.

a fragment of space come back to babble on the edge of space.

on a withdrawal
of languages, today, we will move forward, at times deprived
of language.

the word
going out of words, as it has touched on things, enjoins: speak.

yes, beside, once again,
what at the moment crossed my mind.

"so, you'll be the numbskull of your thought."

space.   a fragment of space, separated — as from one word
to another, when both of them together will be crossed
— by separation.

the fragmentation, I breathe, it disappears, that is space.

a fragment of space.
that can be the anachronic cloud, a fall, a piece of ice, some
water swallowed when thirsty, the wall again, or the level
paving of the road as it abruptly comes to itself, moment of
everything that separates...

. . . .

           dans le rêve, la figure du facteur
à côté de la cheminée, sur le toit, qui fléchit légèrement —
à l'époque de l'éclosion jour après jour de la volute des
liserons — alors que dans la cuisine, où plus d'une lettre
aura été brûlée, le foyer noir reste vide, toute la chaleur se
trouvant dehors.   grandes volutes dans le rêve, longues
volutes des explications entées comme à vide, et qui, prenant
sur le jour à venir — bleu céleste — de se vouloir rapportées
à l'éclaircie éventuelle du réveil, n'auront été, pour à l'instant
se dissiper,   rêve s'ajoutant à rêve,   que pur et simple
prolongement du rêve.

            ne voulant pas omettre la plus petite
part de ce qui doit être perdu aujourd'hui.   c'est
aujourd'hui.   rien n'est perdu.

           la montagne, un regard : perçant
— quand j'ai ouvert les yeux. mots eux aussi à forme de
visage humain dans des yeux sans lesquels jamais encore je
n'aurais entrevu le mien. mots, sur leurs percées — entendre
— apercevoir — prononcer — à forme de visage humain.

facteur.   fumiste.
« mots qui portent avec eux leur place ».   j'attends
un bon moment sur le bord de la route.

. . . .
. . . .

in the dream, the face of the postman
next to the chimney, on the roof, which slightly bends   —
at the time when day after day the morning glories bloom in
a spiral — while in the kitchen, where more than one letter has
been burned, the black hearth sits empty, all the warmth now
outside.   great spirals in the dream, long spirals of comments
grafted as if idly, and which catching on the day to come —
sky-blue — wishing to be carried back to the potential bright-
ness of waking, have been no more, dispersed in a moment,
dream added to dream,   than pure and simple prolongation
of the dream.

not wanting to omit the smallest
part of what today must be lost.   it is
today.   nothing is lost.

the mountain, a gaze: piercing
— once I've opened my eyes. they too are words shaping a
human face in eyes without which I would never yet have
glimpsed my own face. words, when they pierce through — hearing
— perceiving — pronouncing — shape a human face.

postman.   slacker.
"words that carry their place with them."   I wait
quite a while at the edge of the road.

. . . .
. . . .

depuis pas mal d'années,
à dévaler la côte de St Maurice, et croisant, peu avant
d'atteindre le fond, l'inconnu habitant la maison en bordure
du ruisseau jusqu'à laquelle le soleil ne vient pas, occupé
toujours à élargir, en rognant dans la pente, une parcelle
plantée d'arbres fruitiers, de la main au passage, de la tête,
j'échange avec lui un signe — sans qu'il y ait lieu de freiner.

parole en moins sur fond de français.

mais chaque fois la jubilation
d'être — la parole qui n'aura pas été prononcée, exultante,
comportant elle aussi sa place   — en avant des mots
brièvement.

le support abrupt — d'une parole à une autre — lui aussi
façonne.

j'ai oublié le français. un instant, retrouver, hors de la langue
à nouveau, le français.

. . . .
.

il se sera —
dans l'alignement de la parole, et de l'une à l'autre, creusé
comme une assiette.   pour faire place — dès le centre
momentané pareil au visage médian ou une assiette—
comme après soi encore.

qui est en suspens, le vide, comme une assiette.

for all these years,
hurtling down the hill of St. Maurice, and coming across,
shortly before I reach the bottom, the unknown inhabitant
of the house bordering the stream, a house untouched by the
sun, always busy enlarging, as he cuts into the slope, a parcel
of land planted with fruit-trees, with my hand, with my head,
passing by I exchange a greeting — with no need for brakes.

one word fewer against the backdrop of French.

but each time the jubilation
of being — the word which won't be pronounced, exultant,
it too bringing along its place   —   ahead of words
briefly.

the steep support   — from one word to another — it also
shapes.

I've forgotten French. a moment, to find again, outside the
language once more, French.

. . . .

a kind of fold —
in the alignment of the words, and from one to the other,
will be hollowed out.   to make room   — from the
momentary center not unlike the median face or a fold —
as after itself again.

which is in suspense, the void, like a fold.

les mots
ne se seront pas refermés sur-le-champ.

ce mot n'aura pas été le mot
juste.   mais je suis à côté.

avant d'avoir saisi, j'ai entendu.   je ne saisis pas.

demeure, le mot — sur l' attention qui traverse — ouvert.

une pierre.   casser la
pierre — réfractaire — il y aura plusieurs pierres.

une pierre.

parole fractale.   parole de face.

le défaut : le futur   ce que je n'ai pas saisi,
pourtant ne m'est pas étranger — ni la langue inconnue
tout à fait, puisque la parole, s'y hasardant, trouvera là sa
fraîcheur informe.

words

will not be closed back up right away.

this word was not the right

one.   but I'm next to it.

before I grasped, I heard.   I do not grasp.

remaining, the word — on the attention that traverses it —open.

a stone.   break the

stone — refractory — there will be several stones.

a stone.

fractal word.   word face-on.

the flaw: the future.   what I haven't grasped,
is yet not foreign to me — nor the language completely
unknown, since the word, venturing there, will find its
unformed freshness.

dans la parole, ce point attenant à autre chose — chose, non parole encore — qui, sur l'instant, restera ouverte comme enclavée dans ce qui plus loin peut-être dit.

                                    un regard
n'est pas étranger à ce qui a été dit, la lettre étant toujours augurale.

.   .   .   .

un blanc. une pierre.   quelqu'un. un mot : que, sur la
                        rupture, ou l'interruption,
           je trouve le départ une seconde fois.   là, je
                                    bute.

                        l'inerte : indice de la matérialité de
ce mot pris de court dans l'instant où il rejoint le dehors
cessant de donner prise.   trop
rapide.   mais les mots, de même que le
dehors, se dérobent.   opaque
ou limpide, ce sera la même épaisseur.   ce surcroît
momentané d'une épaisseur de matière de mot dans le mot,
dès lors que par son travers — de tout le poids qui est le sien
et pour dire l'absence de pesanteur — a, dans l'épaisseur
commune, parlé le support.

                        il ne parle que si,
enfin — et comme il supporte, je suis, un instant, parvenu
moi-même à être là.

in the word, this point bordering something else — thing,
not yet word — which, for the moment, will remain open
as if inserted into what, further on, perhaps says.

                                                    a gaze
isn't foreign to what's been said, the letter being always
augural.

.   .   .   .

a blank.   a stone.   someone.   a word: on the
                     rupture, or interruption, let me
                 find the outset a second time.   there, I
                               stumble.

                         the inert: clue to the materiality of
this word caught out in the moment when it rejoins the outside
ceasing to allow a grip.   too
quick.   but words, the same as
the outside, shy away.   opaque
or clear, the thickness remains the same.   this momentary
surfeit of a thickness of word-matter within the word, as
soon as abeam to it — with all the weight it musters and
to say the absence of gravity — the support has, in the
common thickness, spoken.

                              it speaks only if,
at last — and as it supports, I have, for a moment, managed
to be there myself.

matière torrentielle,
et, à première vue, sans avoir bougé, qui — plus rapide que
les mots de la langue, a été le support des mots.

de son support passager, la parole se sera incorporée quelque
chose, quitte — demeurée ouverte alors, à se découvrir en
défaut. comme soi, route, papier.

prêtant l'oreille
à ce que la route n'aura pas voituré, ce que la parole n'a pas
pu dire.

sur une attente interrompue, puisque la langue
trouvera corps dans une attente, j'ai — sans le soutenir alors,
atteint à ce qui est hors de la langue.

fraîcheur
— et la traversée — de ce qui pré-existe, dégagé comme
futur.

le français.   la fraîcheur.

mots
de la langue, comme des traces de la terre.   épars.

la fraîcheur — un vestige.
. . . .
. . . .

                                 torrential matter,
and, at first sight, not having moved, which — quicker than
the words of the language, has been the words' support.

from its temporary support, the word has incorporated
something even — remaining open then, has discovered
itself caught off guard. like oneself, road, paper.

                                   lending an ear
to what the road hasn't conveyed, what the word hasn't been
able to say.

        on an interrupted expectancy, since the language
will find its body in an expectancy, I've — without sustaining
it then, attained what is beyond the language.

                                   freshness
— and the crossing over — of what preexists, freed as
future.

French.   freshness.

                                     words
of the language, like tracks of the earth.   scattered.

freshness — a vestige.

. . . .
. . . .

plus avant, aussi bien,
puisqu'il faut s'interrompre. que, de l'un à l'autre aussi, on
doit interrompre.   mais
la langue initiale, la langue qu'ici et là j'ai vu devancer la
mienne, la langue étrangère — langue à l'infini hors —
figurera aussi ce qui en soi inhumé aura pu ne pas en être une
encore.

                                                        vestiges
dans les constructions de nos langues de remplois et de
vestiges comme autant de trouées d'un avenir informe qui,
plus loin ou plus haut, dans sa fraicheur, est signifié sous les
yeux.

les temps d'arrêt qu'elle emporte avec elle, s'impriment dans
la langue comme du jour.

le français.   il me reste encore à traduire du français.

on ne s'aperçoit pas que *cela* n'a pas été traduit.

further, especially since
we must interrupt ourselves. since, one to another as well,
we must interrupt.   but
the initial language, the language I've seen here and there
move ahead of my own, the foreign language — language
endlessly outside — will also stand for what interred in
itself might not have been one yet.

vestiges
in the constructions of our languages of re-uses and vestiges
like so many breaches of an unformed future which,
further or higher, in its freshness, is signified before our
eyes.

the pauses it carries with it are imprinted in the language
like day.

French.   I still need to translate from French.

we don't notice: *that* has not been translated.

Dérapage sur une plaque de verglas, déchet de la neige

Citations de Jean Tortel, à qui ces pages sont dédiées.

Tombe la foudre
Chaque fois que.

                                              tomber : comme de la
phrase transcrite, un mot en route aura pu tomber :   là aussi
                                                    cela ouvre,
              éclairant.

cela, qui n'est pas tombé encore   —   et même ne tombera pas,
ici demeure en suspens.

                                              une chute.   sans
moi   —   qui de nouveau obstrue, elle ne peut avoir lieu.

Skidding on a patch of ice, snow's waste

Quotations from Jean Tortel, to whom these pages are dedicated.

Lightning falls
Each time that.

                                                 to fall : like the
transcribed sentence, a word on its way might fall :   there also
                                       it opens,
              shedding light.

this word, that has not yet fallen — and even will not fall — is
held here in suspense.

                                      a fall.   without
me — who obstructs yet again — this couldn't have happened.

apport du mot en instance comme un timbre produit avant le sens.   et, dans un tel instant, c'est le sens — pareil à une chute.   sur sa rétrodiction.

le sens est en avant   comme debout.

                                        il aura fallu
      appliquer l'oreille à la route.

mordre de la poussière, autrement.

                              « derrière chaque phrase,
il y a une histoire. » — « ce n'est pas l'histoire qui m'aura
retenu.   ni même une phrase : la phrase en soi
ne me retiendra pas. »   — « la chute, alors. »   — « le
papier.   là, à la place de la phrase.   ponctuant
toujours.   et — être debout. »

                        « dire que je suis debout, je ne
le peux pas, sans pouvoir tomber également : c'est la phrase. »

bringing words like a tone produced before
meaning.   and, at such a moment, it is
meaning — similar to a fall.   on its retrodiction.

the meaning is ahead.   as if standing.

you'll need to put
your ear to the road.

or else chew the dust.

'behind each sentence,
there's a story.'   — 'it's not the story that
interests me.   or even a sentence: the sentence in itself
doesn't interest me.'   — 'the fall, then.'   — 'the
paper.   there, in place of the sentence.   always
interspersed.   and — standing.'

'I cannot say I'm standing, unless I'm
equally able to fall : that is the sentence.'

cramer.　　　　　　　　　　déraper dans la langue
— où elle-même la langue ne cesse de déraper.

ou bien ça crame.

le sol — du genou jusqu'aux dents de la tête — est là.

　　　　　　　　　　sur un point comme tangent à
l'écart trop prolongé pour être perceptible, la foudre porte.
la foudre de la langue.　　　　　　　ici le présent,
　　　　　　une fraction de temps, rétabli.

un mot — une fraction du temps — en moins, et l'articulation
disparue.　　　　　　　　　　il complétera.

　　　　　　　　　　　　la phrase,
en se rompant :　« ce qui est, n'est pas tenable ».　pour
　　　　　　　peu que dans la phrase conductrice
passe ce qui, la relation traversée, un instant illuminera
dehors.　　　　　　ce qui est : de nouveau
le présent, énonciation révoquée.　　　que, là, cela
ne soit pas tenable composera la phrase.　— « mais
la phrase est rompue ».　　— « rien n'aura manqué ».

dans la phrase, je vois un instant le papier.

　　　　　　　　　« je vois ce que je vois ».
le mot manquant, de nouveau j'ai vu.

incinerate   to skid in language
where even language itself ceaselessly skids.

or even incinerates.

the ground — from your knees to the teeth in your head — is there.

on a point like a tangent to
the gap too drawn out to be perceived, the lightning door.
the lightning of language.   here the present,
                    a fraction of time, is restored.

a word — a fraction of time — any less, and the articulation
disappears.   it will complete.

the sentence,
shattering: 'what is, isn't bearable.'   as long as
                    something passes through the conductive
sentence that can, having traversed the connection, for a moment light
up the outside.   what is: again
the present, enunciation cast off.   it won't
be bearable to compose a sentence, there.   — 'but
the sentence is shattered.'   — 'nothing will be missed.'

in the sentence, I see the paper for a moment.

'I see what I see.'
missing the word, I saw anew.

cramer. mot de l'incinération irréalisable, charogne et plastiques confondus, de la décharge sauvage aujourd'hui.   là, dans sa fraîcheur d'étymologie, se laissera — si l'on prête l'oreille, percevoir — *cremare* — la crépitation du mot ancien assourdie momentanément, clair et vif.   le mot du déchet de la langue une fois encore avisé, comme aveugle sur l'instant :   la ressource.   la source aux endroits
                            du déchet non dégradable.

. . . .
. . . .
. . . .

Crète.   *Golden Beach.*   rouleaux limpides comme intouchés du détritus qu'ils voiturent sans relâche jusqu'à la plage matelassée, putréfaction indissociable de l'imputrescible.   plus loin, le fil d'une ligne de pêcheur immergé dans la frange de la tache rouge diluée en brun dont l'auréole se perd dans le bleu absolu en contrebas de l'abattoir de campagne :   taureau aux flancs boueux stationnaire à la porte.   absolu :   l'eau est limpide, absolument opaque.

incinerate. word for an unrealizable cremation, carcass and plastics mixed up, from today's savage dump.   there, in the freshness of its etymology, there will remain — if you lend it your ear, for a moment you'll sense — *incinerare* — the muffled, crackling breath of the ancient word, clear and alive.   the word from language's dump aware once again, like a blind man for an instant: the resource.   the source for places
                    of undegradable waste.

. . . .
. . . .
. . . .

Crete.   *Golden Beach.* translucent rolls as if untouched by the waste they convey without reprieve all the way to the carpeted beach, what rots indivisible from what does not.   further on, the thread of a fishing line submerged in the fringe of the red stain diluted to brown, its halo lost in the absolute blue below the rural slaughterhouse :   mud-flanked bull standing at the door.   absolute :   the water is clear, absolutely opaque.

1966

                                             écrit
sous le réflecteur de la montagne enneigée qui dans
l'absence de soleil produit le jour

montagne en surplomb de la table de noyer sur laquelle
viennent d'être tracés des mots, comme sur le plateau de la
table la lumière de la neige écorche le papier

place faite — comme jour — est-ce, là, savoir ?

au terme de ce qui se cherche à dire, un évidement nouveau
— sans voir où il doit conduire — comme en relief
se produit face à soi brusquement

                                    pressentiment rafraîchi
lorsque venant sur soi l'intact a refermé

le relief — la montagne   le réflecteur de la montagne

eaux libres dans leur boîtier de glace

1966

                                 written
under the reflector, the snowy mountain, that in the sun's
absence gives rise to day

mountain that overhangs the walnut table where words
have just been traced, as on the tabletop the snow's light
skins the paper alive

making room — like daylight — is, that, to know?

at the end of what we try to say, a new hollowing-out
— without seeing where it must lead — as in relief
abruptly arises before us

                               renewed intuition
when approaching us the intact has closed again

the relief — the mountain   the reflector of the mountain

free waters in their casing of ice

          le jour qui n'a pas été rejoint
descend par longues coulées implacables

tout apparaît à notre place, l'emplacement alors apparaît

            constriction du lieu
où l'on a pu mettre pied

majoration de l'espace comme amenuisement soudain

la montagne en *réalité*, sur le retrait de qui l'aura dessinée
           (je la vois
      par grêles de paillettes blanches ou
      clairières de nouveau
   criblant le volume gris d'une cendre qui souffle
entre soi et le feu du papier)   c'est ce qui, démesuré,
se dresse devant quiconque peut avoir prescience du
resserrement consécutif à sa disparition

la montagne en réalité

montagne ou carafe ou visage

       the daylight that has not been reached
descends in long implacable flows

everything appears in place of us, location then appears

                           shrinking of the place
where we've set foot

increase of space as a sudden narrowing

the mountain in *reality*, when whoever drew it is removed
                    (I see it
             through hails of white specks or
               clearings once more
        riddling the gray volume of an ash that blows
between me and the paper's fire)   that is what,
unbounded, rises up before whoever has foreknowledge of
the closing-in that follows our disappearance

the mountain in reality

mountain or water-jug or face

oui, air — et résolution
de la parole dans l'insignifiant, l'air

le chemin qui ne précède pas
tant que j'avance a tout d'un coup cédé

ciel rugueux, comme il laissera sans ciel,
respiré

toi, toute poussière   tout à toi dans la poussière

poussiéreuse
avancée, comme corde dans le souffle

à la fin du jour, porte refermée sur le vent dehors

1967

                                        yes, air — and resolution
of speech in the meaningless, the air

                                    the path that doesn't precede
as much as I advance has suddenly ceded

                            rugged sky, as it will leave without sky,
breathed

you, all dust   all to yourself in the dust

                                                            dusty
advance, like a rope in my breathing

at the end of day, door closed on the wind outside

1968

distance me sera rendue où je me romps

ici je veux — murmure ininterrompu du torrent —
terminer   ici je veux

                    montagne — vouloir
et vouloir demeuré en retrait à nouveau des grands souffles
vouloir aride   ce qui
          n'est pas en retrait aura disparu, et
nous-mêmes ici

                              entamé
par ce qui est au-devant de moi, cela, déjà, est avancer
                              parmi le vent circulaire,
comme faux à venir, au ras du sol déjà

                              je vois,
je vais — en mouvement sous le ciel après moi

chemin, le jour, ferré   ciel de nuit clouté

1968

distance will be given back to me or I'll break

here I want — the torrent's uninterrupted murmur —
to end   here I want

                              mountain — wanting
and wanting to stay withdrawn anew from the great breaths
arid wanting   what is
            not withdrawn will have disappeared, and
ourselves here

                                                  cut into
by what is ahead of me, that, already, is to move forward
                              among the circular wind,
like a scythe to come, already flush with the ground

                                                  I see,
I go — moving under the sky after me

day, iron-clad path   hobnailed night-sky

                              à travers l'éclatement des traits
le visage inconnu de retour comme reconnu

                                     efficacité de la pesée du
vide du ciel comme empêchement à tracer sur le moment le
mot qui succédera

chaînes de rosée

                                   maintenir le vide,
réserver — alors que la masse excessive comprime —
l'emplacement vide pour qu'en avant de soi quelque chose
revienne à découvert

susciter cet emplacement comme respirer

                                     sous la pesée du ciel
                                          vide
comme envol ou trouée

lointain en distance se rapproche ou se résout, tel que
visage dans la chaleur

            through the explosion of features
the unknown face coming back as if recognized

                   effective, the weight of the
sky's emptiness, as it prevents us from tracing for the moment
the word that will follow

chains of dew

              maintain the emptiness,
preserve — while the enormous mass compresses —
the empty location so that ahead of you something comes
back open again

kindle this location like breathing

                  under the empty sky's
                    weight
as if flying or piercing through

far-off distance comes closer or resolves, like
a face in the heat

     ... par masses aujourd'hui de
journaux sous le bras ou autour de lui, se serait-il assis
pour devenir — dans les bas-côtés ou la marge, sous le
ciel, lui-même nuage, ou la marge de nouveau

le sourd-muet, bras écartés, au milieu de l'attroupement
silencieux, comme sorti de sa réclusion et pour la première
fois descendu alors jusqu'à la chaussée, sautant sur place,
faisant sur place de grands bonds, criant, et désignant (?)
avec des mots inarticulés les détonations qui se succèdent au
loin

     à soi : retour à un lieu de départ,
mais le lieu même en déplacement

intonations de la vie qui jamais ne dépose

       hauteur en silence
répond aux alignements de ce qui s'écrit   répond
     de toutes parts

           ... today through masses of
newspapers under his arm or around him, could he have
sat down to become   —   by the roadsides or the margin,
under the sky, himself a cloud, or the margin once more

the deaf-mute, arms thrown wide, in the middle of the
silent crowd, as if emerging from his reclusion and then
for the first time coming out to the sidewalk, hopping up
and down, bounding up and down, and shouting (?)
with inchoate words pointing toward the detonations
going off in the distance

           back to ourselves : return to a place of
departure, though the place itself is displaced

intonations of life that never slackens

                   height in silence
answers the alignments of what is written   answers
                from every side

1970

dans le mot le silence — et,
par trouée dans les trames conductrices jusqu'à silence tel
qu'à vue
de la chose même   jusqu'au silence le cri perçant de
l'hirondelle

1970

<pre>
                              in the word, silence — and,
        through the hole in the conductive weft through to silence
                                              as to sight of
        the thing itself   through to silence, the piercing cry
        of the swallow
</pre>

le froid — saveur, chaque fois
de ce qui finit   de l'achevé en fleur
comme   à extrémité de souffle   la vocalise

eau trop violente, où
je fais halte, pour être bue

air
davantage mordu que respiré

cela passe du pain aux mots

arrivé de partout,
partout retrouvé devant soi

je n'ai pas pesé sur l'article

soleil
parti à l'ouest, l'ouest lui-même est parti

1971

                        the cold — a taste, each time
of what ends   from full flowering
like   with the last of breath   song

                        water too violent, where
I stop, to drink

                                          air
more bitten than breathed

that passes from bread to words

                        arrived from everywhere,
found everywhere in front of you

I didn't stress the article

                                          sun
departed to the west, the west itself has departed

                              sens tout d'un coup sans article

apparu debout

ce qui s'imprimera reste taillé dans la soif

                                          éclat

tel qu'à une face s'ajustera l'air froid

traduire   j'arrive du dehors,
et   —   mot du dehors dans la langue qui n'est pas la
mienne, dans votre propre langue   la langue qui par
instants sera la mienne aujourd'hui, pourtant, comme je
serai venu à vous

rauschen   mot du bruit hors de la langue, tel que dans
votre langue Hölderlin l'a prononcé

ce mot désignant le bruit que le vent fait parmi les branches
ou dans le blé

                                     dans la langue
comme de l'autre côté de la langue

                meaning suddenly without an article
appearing upright

what will be printed remains carved into thirst

                                          burst
like a face adjusting to cold air

to translate   I arrive from outside,
and   —   word from outside in the language that isn't
mine, in your own language   the language that at
moments will be mine today, nonetheless, as I will have
come to you

rauschen   word for a sound outside language, such
as Hölderlin uttered it in your language

this word signifies the sound made by the wind among
branches or in wheat

                                     in language
as from the other side of language

           terre s'élargissant sous la foulée
jusqu'à une tête qui découvrira peut-être,
             et que ciel comme papier ou parole
    emporte

le mot du bruit — *rauschen*   parmi vous, je n'ai pas à
le traduire, étant ici

de l'autre côté de la langue, il y a une autre langue

moi-même — arrivé aujourd'hui de l'autre côté, et qui
pour vous n'aurai aussi été d'abord que bruit

dans le temps de l'entre-temps   —   muet comme il
s'incorpore, une parole se rompt, une parole se prépare

           au hasard confondant qui de chacun
de nous aura fait homme de telle langue plutôt que de
l'autre, quelque chose de rudimentaire qui isole sans être
saisi, distinctement se refuse :   poésie

              earth expanding underfoot
up to a head that will uncover perhaps,
              and that sky like paper or speech
     carries away

the word of the sound — *rauschen*   among you, I don't
have to translate it, being here

on the other side of language, there's another language

myself — come today from the other side, and who
for you at first would have also been only sound

in the time between time — mute as it takes shape,
a word is broken, a word is prepared

               mingling with chance
which has made of each of us a person of this language
rather than that, something elemental that isolates without
being grasped, and distinctly refuses :   poetry

Congère

le poids
celui que j'ai oublié
mais
le poids.

.

y a-t-il
ralentissement

fallait-il
vite

encore
aller vite.

mais
le souffle
que tu ne retiens pas
est

le tien
quand tu respires.

Snowdrift

the weight
the one I've forgotten
but
      the weight.

    •

   is there
      slowing down

did we need
hastily

        again
to make haste.

        but
   the breath
      you don't hold back
  is

yours
when you breathe.

                                                    d'être

allés comme, confondus terre et le ciel,
            ensemble ils s'éclipsent, l'un à l'autre.

                                        et la charnière

détachée.

pas sec   —   c'est le mot que retenait le vent.

            ce que j'ai face à moi
            je
            ne l'ai pas.

•

            c'est

            et

            asséchant
                la sécheresse

                                to have
gone as, earth and sky merged,
           they eclipse each other.

                           and the hinge
undone.

not dry — is the word the wind retained.

           what I have in front of me
           I
           do not have.

                ·

           it is

           and

           drying up
              the drought

•

elle-même
           comme aplanie
venue à bout
de l'un
              déjà.

et le mot   —   desserrant.

ce que j'ai vu
est gardé par les eaux.

pur
       l'inespéré
même
sous les yeux.

•

the drought itself
      as though ironed out
finished up
already
      with the one.

and the word   —   loosening.

                          what I've seen
is kept by the waters.

pure
      the unhoped-for
even
before our eyes.

j'ai
bloqué sur déplacement de monde

sur
de l'eau

ou le bleu sitôt comme

encouru.

                            le vent
pas distrait de son refus du vent.

        je vois la route   —   entre nous la route
et la part de soi
        dont sans se séparer on doit se détacher encore,
                comme entre nous
plus loin la route sans paupière.

I can't
get past the shifting world

past
the water

or the blue as soon as

incurred.

                                        the wind
not deterred by its rebuff of the wind.

     I see the road   —   between us the road
and the part of ourselves
        we must leave behind without yet giving up,
                 as between us
further on, the road without eyelids.

                              tu ouvres, il faut

passer.

                       la porte des montagnes, où

elle éclaire, a claqué.

             la neige.   j'ai coupé par la neige,

je n'ai pas coupé.

               les images arrondies ont disparu.

                    montagne
                    à la recherche de ses lèvres

                    chambre inoccupée compacte
                    après
                            chambre

                    descendue

                            puis
                  rapportée.

you open, we must
pass.

the door of the mountains, where
it sheds light, has slammed shut.

the snow.   I cut through the snow,
I did not cut.

the rounded images have disappeared.

mountain
searching for its lips

unoccupied room, compact
after
         room

lowered

then
brought back.

air

                        arrêté
comme respiré

centre
respiratoire alors

atteint

sur

un
escarpement

devant soi
l'air
                              droit

comme

sans mémoire montagne
rapportée

                                    à

l'air

droit.

air

                    stopped
as if breathed

respiratory
center then

struck

on

a
cliff

before us
the straight
                         air

as

mountain without memory
brought back

                              to

the straight

air.

Luzerne

Étant là

membres
ou
mots

mais sur un bras
j'ai débordé

comme le vent.

Alfalfa

Being here

limbs
or
words

but on an arm
I've brimmed over

like the wind.

J'aime
la hauteur qu'en te parlant
j'ai prise
sans avoir

pied.

Mots

en avant de moi
la blancheur de l'inconnu
où
je les place
est

amicale.

Comme élargi au-delà de sa
langue
respirer

perdu.

I love
the height I've taken
speaking to you
without touching

bottom.

Words

in front of me
the whiteness of the unknown
where
I place them
is

friendly.

As if enlarged beyond one's
language
breathing

lost.

Pour toi
        comme la neige.

avant qu'il ait neigé.

Montagne

que je ramène
à moi

pour passer dehors.

J'ai dormi
dans l'épaisseur du battant.

Pas d'air
qui ne soit rompu

et

air venir

scinder.

For you
        as the snow.

before it has snowed.

Mountain

I bring back
to me

to go outside.

I've slept
in the thickness of the door.

No air
that isn't broken

and

air to come

split apart.

Feu

sans la pesanteur
du froid
de ce qui reste à brûler.

Que
reste dans ma vertèbre
la brusquerie

debout.

Fire

without the weight
of the chill
of what's yet to burn.

May
the brusqueness
stay in my vertebra

upright.

L'asphalte

où
            rafales de
    l'immobile

            de même et
par

des plages
ici.

Asphalt

where
     gusts of
   immobility

     same as and
by

beaches
here.

dans
le buis

comme l'abrupt
le
labour produit le vent

briller

tel
qu'
ici de nouveau et pour
toujours

perdu.

in
    the boxwood

like the drop-off
tilling
generates wind

shine

               as
if
   here is newly and
forever

        lost.

            le bleu
admirable
le
bleu

        comme violent

et
      l'asphalte.

the lovely
blue
the
blue

as if violent

and
the asphalt.

« *Ca – va – lari – a – a – a – na …* »

Ca – va – lari – a – a – a – na
        appel,
                                       à l'arrêt, du conducteur
qui a cultivé l'élongation   démesurée de l'ongle de son
petit doigt   lieu-dit,
un cri

mot dans l'espace   mot espacé, emportant avec soi
                                comme il se sera espacé
                quelques parcelles de la durée du trajet pour
ouvrir soudain sur la mer du golfe

une seule voile blanche près de Ca – va – lari – a – a –
a – na

                                       route
qui s'attarde sur la dernière syllabe de la vocalise de
l'arrivée

'Ca – va – lari – a – a – a – na ...'

Ca – va – lari – a – a – a – na
       call

                                  at the stop, by the conductor
who cultivated the excessive   growth of his
pinkie nail   local place,
a shout

word in space   spaced word, bringing along
                                      since it will be spaced
                          some parcels of the trip's duration to
open suddenly on the sea of the gulf

a single white sail near Ca – va – lari – a – a –
a – na

                                           road
that lingers on the last syllable of the arrival's
song

carnet perdu peut-être, le monde aura cessé d'être
couvert

                                          à la chaux, du
sel pour la pérennité de l'enduit

buanderie   bergerie

                    toute la charge, sur eux des mots
ici la reprennent sans certitude qu'ils pourront
                                  l'accepter

                             plusieurs vies blanches
soudées par de la chaux

              les mots de la langue que je ne connais pas brûlent
                    un peu au-dessous des yeux

notebook lost perhaps, the world will cease to be
covered

                                                with whitewash, some
salt for the plaster's durability

folded laundry   sheepfold

                           the whole burden, here
words take it up again without certainty they can
                                       shoulder it

                                   several whitened lives
bonded by whitewash

                   the words of the language I don't know burn
                              a bit below the eyes

« Coquelicots... »

<blockquote>coquelicots,</blockquote>

la récolte rouge — tomates mûres, plutôt, et silence
à ma semelle

<blockquote>que d'une montagne
à l'autre, de même que d'un mot à un autre, le vide,
de l'un à l'autre porteur à son tour
du vide, ici se soulève, comme respirer</blockquote>

entre deux vides, celui-ci — avant qu'il s'en arrache,
tout de même fiché

<blockquote>dans quel mortier</blockquote>

aura pour le plafond été noyé jambage

<blockquote>ou pilier</blockquote>

la marge passe au centre sans caractères d'impression

'Poppies...'

                                          poppies,
the red harvest — ripe tomatoes, rather, and silence
under my sole

                        from one mountain
           to the other, as one word to another, the void,
                  each lifting the void in turn, here lifting
           itself, as if breathing

between two voids, this one — before tearing itself away,
stuck all the same

                              in which mortar
for the ceiling post or pillar will

                                be drowned

           the margin passes to the center without print

« Alors que je passe... »

<blockquote>

                                              alors que je passe
devant les volets de la maison,
                               de nouveau quelque chose
  pour effacer passe comme main sur le front

</blockquote>

<blockquote>

                                       du sommeil,
pas grand-chose — sinon, de nouveau, sur son
interruption, à retenir   comme fibre,
et fibre, chaque fois, de ce qui une fois encore se
pourrait, passant de substance de sommeil à substance
d'éveillé, sans sur l'une ou sur l'autre la saisie la plus
infime

</blockquote>

<blockquote>

                                     disposition
des fibres d'une matière de sommeil demeurant,
comme toujours, à saisir   quelle que soit la langue,
par l'autre, à saisir toujours

</blockquote>

<blockquote>

                                     carton
glissé dans le livre que j'aurai traduit, glacé, lecture
suspendue, par glacier

</blockquote>

<blockquote>

                                     affranchi
l'arrivée autant que de départ

</blockquote>

'When I pass...'

                                           when I pass

before the shutters of the house,

                              once again something passes

to erase like a hand over the brow

                                      of sleep,

not much — except, again, upon its

interruption, to retain   like fiber,

and fiber, each time, of what might be possible one more

time, passing from substance of sleep to substance of

wakefulness, without on one or the other the slightest

grasp

                                    arrangement

of the fibers of sleep's matter still needing,

as always, to be grasped   whatever the language,

by the other, always to be grasped

                                      card

slipped into the book I translated, frozen, reading

suspended, by glacier

                                    freed

from arrival as well as departure

                                        sol du rêve
comme abrégé, quand sur le point de me rendormir,
il culmine, sol rêvé

                                au signet qui marque, où
                                        je l'aurai
glissé, lieu blanc sans lettre

je me suis trop souvent trouvé sur mon chemin

dream's ground
as if abridged, when I'm about to doze off again,
it culminates, dreamed-of ground

with the bookmark that marks, where
I slipped it
in, a blank space without letters

I've found myself too often on my path

« *Langage n'attend pas...* »

                                                      langage n'attend pas

qu'il se trace

à la limite le trait lui-même aura disparu

                 le mot, si on sort,
se laissera figurer sur le seuil

                                          terre
qu'à la bouche aussi je pourrai avoir — comme rien,
                 l'ayant sous les pieds

                     matière de mot, la tienne également,
comme chose sans voix qu'en retour le mot frappant a
éclairée

                                         une

meule de perceptions

                                 allant à la meule
comme à soi rapporter le soleil, *de la dimension*
                               d'un pied d'homme

'Language does not wait...'

                                      language does not wait
to be traced

in the end the stroke itself will have vanished

                                   the word, if we leave,
will let us sketch it on the threshold

                                          earth
that I could also have in my mouth — as nothing,
                 having it under my feet

                              word-matter, yours too,
as a voiceless thing that in turn the striking word has
illumined

                                               a

grindstone of perceptions

                                going to the grindstone
as if bringing us back the sun, *the size*
                        of a man's foot

« Une chose... »

une chose,
le nom qui est le sien ne la recouvre pas

oubli, saveur du rien

où a disparu la dernière trace de
chemin, terrassiers qui chantent en contrebas,
cassant
des pierres   o — i — o

n'importe où, pour
sortir aussitôt

s u é e
d'images qui, s'étant faite nuage, a soudain envahi le
jour, comme en pleine nuit un peu du jour

eau prenant le ciel

soutenir, supporter, ou
annuler (recouvrir) — et même emporter, tour à tour
laisseront sourdre un sens, le
même à peu près

sur grands dépôts de monde
debout l'instant de fonte comme il a pris le dessus

'A thing...'

                                        a thing,
the name attached to it no longer covers it

oblivion, taste of nothing

                where the last trace of the path has
disappeared, road-workers who sing down below,
                                        breaking
        stones   o — e — o

                                no matter where, to
get out of here

                                        s w e a t
of images that turned into a cloud, has suddenly engulfed
the day, as in the thick of night a bit of daylight

water taking the sky

                                sustain, support, or
annul (cover again) — and even sweep away, by turns
                        will let a meaning well up, the
same more or less

                        upright on great sediments of world
the moment of thawing has taken the upper hand

« Jubilation... »

                                    jubilation
de rapaces criant comme ils plongent dans l'épaisseur
du ciel, trois, puis quatre à nouveau
                              criant

                              carrière en face,
vide aujourd'hui dans le versant — une scarification

socle des synclinaux, brusque torsion des parallèles
pierreux qui se chevauchent

                              racas rentrant
dans le silence prolongé de la page, silence lui-même
devenue *le fracas*

                                    face à soi
matière à route puisée

                              papier sur cela,
tranquillité du papier, quand, par les terres rompues,
                              j'ai moi-même pu reprendre

                    de l'agrégat des ans — compact,
fracture du temps a fait un mot

'Jubilation...'

jubilation
of raptors screeching as they plunge into the thickness
of the sky, three, then four again,
screeching

across from me, the
quarry empty today on the mountainside — a scarring

base of the synclines, abrupt torsion of overlapping
rocky parallels

brawl reentering
the prolonged silence of the page, silence itself
becoming *the brawl*

facing yourself
material for the road laid down

paper laid down
paper's tranquility, when, through the broken lands,
I was able to take myself back

from the aggregate of years — compact,
time's fracture formed a word

elle-même la durée fera tache   *spots*
of time (Wordsworth)

instants   taches du temps   lui-même, le temps,
                                                une tache, ou,
par instants, *sous-sol nerveux* libre encore de tout ce qui
pourra s'y apposer, aveugle, par la suite entaché

irisation des labours, grands sols du ciel

                                                à monde
que tu parviennes à t'adosser, sitôt tu le reconnais
devant toi

            bossellements du bleu sur le bord de l'océan
de l'air qu'aucun lit ne borne

villages à odeur de pain sûri

duration itself will leave a stain   *spots*
of time (Wordsworth)

moments   spots of time   time itself
                                                    a spot, or,
at moments, *a nervous undercurrent* freed from all that
could adhere to it, blind, afterwards stained

iridescence of tilling, great soils of the sky

                                        to the world
you lean against, as soon as you recognize it
before you

                            dents of blue on the ocean's edge
of the air that no bed confines

villages smelling of rancid bread

Essor

Il me reste à trouver un dessin.
Pierre Tal-Coat

face
du papier, comme elle s'envisage.

coup
d'œil : un oiseau, trait initial.   en hauteur la feuille
déployée produira l'envergure.

espace à parcourir
jusqu'à une autre face donne lieu en retour, n'y eût-il pour
l'annoter qu'un trait sans ombre encore — vide puis volume,
et volume en cours, au volume global éclairant.

ce qui s'ouvre, passé le seuil
qu'aura inscrit un trait — lui-même franchi, aussitôt avisé —
c'est face à soi
l'espace sans recto ni verso.

Taking flight

I still have to find a drawing.
Pierre Tal-Coat

face
of the paper, as it envisages itself.

a
glance : a bird, initial stroke.   high up, the outspread
          sheet will generate the wingspan.

· space to roam
until another face makes space in return, even if denoted only
by a still-shadowless stroke — void then volume, and volume
ongoing, lighting up the volume overall.

what opens, past the threshold
was inscribed by a stroke — crossed over, as soon as approached —
          it's before us
          space without front or back.

volume d'air.   volume, subitement.   le
                                                      révolu.

là, d'un coup d'œil , cependant   — avant de passer, ainsi que
                                                         toi-même
                                          je me tiens.

trait libre, sur le moment, d'aller sans le vouloir.

                    ici un support toujours comme terre à ciel
rouverte, et de laquelle   — à plat aussi bien que dressée, en
soi la feuille de papier aura pu être, avant même qu'une main
soit intervenue, déjà la fraîche représentation.

                         le support muet debout,
à peine envisagé, traversera — comme le visage nu, regard
                             ouvert en avant de soi, à
               nouveau peut traverser — des condensations
accidentelles d'image, rapidement.

volume of air.   volume, straightaway.   the
                      achieved.

there, at a glance, nonetheless — before passing on, just like
                                yourself
                  I hold back.

a stroke, free for now to go unwillingly.

                        here a supporting medium always like
earth reopened to the sky, and of which — flat as well as
standing upright, in itself the sheet of paper may have been,
even before a hand intervenes, already the fresh portrayal.

                    the mute upright medium,
as soon as faced, will rapidly cross — as the naked face, gaze
                         open before itself, can
          once more cross — the accidental
boiling-down of images.

le trait momentanément sans nom ayant
en retour, et avant de faire image — sur la terre qui obstrue
et doit éclaircir, lui-même alors le pas.

je supporte la terre.

papier nu pourvoit au fond.

la fraction de globe qu'on arpente
n'attire à chaque coup d'oeil, qu'une face, une fois encore,
qui s'efface.

traversé.   c'est le fond qui se traverse.   c'est le fond
qui traverse.

air en avant du trait aussi bien,
et clarté du papier le prenant de court — jusqu'à air, ou
papier, ou à soi.

the stroke in turn, momentarily unnamed,
before it shapes an image — on the earth that obstructs
and must make clear — has precedence.

I support the earth.

naked paper furnishes the background.

the fraction of globe we
pace out offers but a face, at each glance, that is once more
effaced.

crossed. it's the background that's crossed. it's the background
that crosses.

air ahead of the stroke as well,
and brightness of the paper blindsiding it — up to air, or
paper, or stroke itself.

je vois ce que je vois.   cela,
ici couvert ou lavé, intimant ciel ouvert à qui avance.

                                          un trait,
rien que le trait, suspendu, et le fond en soi rentré
                                          alors égal à soi.

                                          envol
            de goélands à l'aplomb de la feuille blanche,
                        blancs eux-mêmes, si j'ai bien vu,
aura par de tels blancs précipité — essor, et la chute, libres
— et temps, le temps d'un clignement, suspendu — une
tache noire. mais noir lui-même cesse d'être noir, et l'encre
à son tour, localisant l'air parcouru, de faire tache.

                        sous la main, comme levé le trait
en cours, subitement, main aveugle développant le coup d'œil
quand le regard s'est absenté.   long
regard en retour où la main n'a pas à se porter.

I see what I see: that,
here covered or washed, hinting open sky to whoever moves forward.

                                                      a stroke, nothing
but the stroke, suspended, and the background withdrawn into itself
                                                   thus equal to itself.

                                                                  flight
                           of seagulls straight up the white page,
                           white themselves, if I've seen right —
flight and fall, both free — and time, the time of a blink, suspended
— has, through such blanks, distilled a black spot. but black itself
ceases to be black, and the ink in turn, pinpointing the air crossed
through, to make a spot.

                           under the hand, the stroke underway
as if lifted, suddenly, blind hand developing the glance when the
gaze has shifted away.   long
gaze in return where the hand need not go.

étagement,
dans les hauteurs, se rapportant à la clarté d'une face
comme au départ dégagée encore, et sans trace de la trace.
là tu entrevois la profondeur — et toi-même, où un regard
attentif de nouveau s'absentera, toi soustrait à toi — du volume
sans cesse évoqué de l'air.

l'envergure : une tache sans dépôt.   et le blanc — altitude
pareille à un à-plat.

je vois
ce que je vois.

cela, de nouveau, revenant
à soi, cela — pour l'espace, se prononcera : t o i.

inconnu
tutoyé.   reconnu.

                                            levels mounting up,
in the heights, linked to the brightness of a face
as if from the outset still clear, and with no trace of the trace.
there, you glimpse the depth — and yourself, where an attentive
gaze will once again shift away, you removed from you — of
the air's volume unceasingly evoked.

the wingspan : a spot leaving nothing behind. and the blankness
        — altitude similar to lying flat.

                                                   I see
what I see.

                                   that, once again, returning
to itself, that — for the space, will be pronounced : y o u.

                                      the unknown
befriended.   recognized.

mais, là,
ce que je vois, et la peinture — autrement, là, qu'objet —
elle-même demeure.

le coup d'œil:

une incise.

dans la solidité du support
analogue au sol debout, quand à l'envisager
on le rapporte à soi.

il me reste à trouver un dessin.

fraction de terre. fraction de temps. un
instant de terre
sorti du temps comme, mouvement suspendu, moi-même
j'aurai face à cela pu l'envisager.

but there,
what I see, and the painting — there otherwise than an object —
itself remains.

the glance:

an incision.

in the solidity of the medium
analogous to the upright ground, when to envisage it
we relate it to ourselves.

I still have to find a drawing.

fraction of earth.   fraction of time.   a
moment of earth
taken out of time as, movement suspended, I myself,
facing that, may have envisaged it.

inconnu

de nouveau reconnu.

sur le point d'être nommé, ce
qu'on voit ayant pris de court, l'omission du nom
— fraîcheur reconduite — peut, sans faire défaut, de nouveau
s'inscrire dans le temps de la nomination.   cela
fera comme tache ou
jour.

par un sol levé, une tache alors de jour.

le trait ascendant — une montagne   le trait descendant :
c'est le même.

dans l'intervalle — libre, une fraction
de temps —
de ce renversement d'un sens à un autre de temps comme,
sur son demi-tour, fraction plane momentanément
de la terre ici escarpée
en suspens.

unknown
known once more.

on the point of being named,
having blindsided what we see, the omission of the name
— freshness renewed — can, without being missed,
inscribe itself again in the time of naming.   that
will make a spot or
light.

through a raised ground, a spot then of light.

the rising stroke — a mountain.   the falling stroke:
the same.

in the interval — free, a fraction
of time —
of this reversal from one meaning to another of time like,
on its about-turn, a fraction momentarily flat
of the earth here steep
unresolved.

blancheur amortit l'aveuglement.

                                                        futur
localisé comme blanc, et à couvrir sitôt du pied — de la
main, ou l'œil.

                                    inconnu — et qui en retour
éclaire : le blanc, pour un futur, incorporé
de nouveau.   intervalle
                        qui de loin éclaire.

whiteness softens blindness.

future
pinpointed as blank, and to be covered straightaway with the foot
— of the hand, or the eye.

unknown — and which brightens
in return : white, for a future, blended in
once more.   interval
that brightens from afar.

Deux traces vertes

au détour de la route, et sorties de la route, deux traces de
roue dans la terre.   dans la terre
meuble de novembre deux traces, plus vertes que le vert
aujourd'hui de la première percée des semis d'hiver.   mais
tranchant sur la légèreté du vert, là, comme étale, ce qui,
depuis, sur cette trace a pu lever l'emporte sur les traces.
deux traits parallèles partis vers le haut où le souvenir même
du tracteur   —   dont les roues, faisant demi-tour, auront
en tassant la terre retournée suscité plus tard surcroît de
couleur — s'efface à son tour dans le versant monochrome.

du regard, là-dessus, plus d'une fois l'un ou l'autre en
passant se sera arrêté.

plus haut, le vert est retranché du vert.

                              ici, vert a traversé une trace.

rien ne manque quand tout a disparu.   choses,
lorsqu'elles reviennent, quelque chose déjà commence à manquer.

                                                le sol
qu'on a eu sous le pied, seul tout à coup   —   sur un
élargissement de l'attention dans l'instant où, semble-t-il,
elle se dissipe — à se voir lui-même porté en direction du
point où, vert ne tranchant plus sur le vert, toutes les
absences se trouvent abrogées ou suspendues.

Two green tracks

at the bend of the road, and leaving the road, two wheel-tracks in the ground.　　　　　in November's loose soil two tracks, greener than the green of winter seedlings' first sprouts today. but cutting across the lightness of the green, there, like spreading water, what has risen on the track in the meantime has prevailed over the tracks. two parallel strokes heading uphill where the very memory of the tractor —making a U-turn, its wheels, in packing down the upturned soil, later brought forth an abundance of color — is lost in turn in the monochrome slope.

looking at it, more than once, one or the other, going by, may have stopped.

further up, the green is cut away from green.

　　　　　　　　　　here, green crossed a track.

nothing is missing when all has disappeared.　　　things: as soon as they return, something begins to be missed.

　　　　　　　　　　　　　the ground you have underfoot, suddenly alone　—　in a widening of attention just when it seems to dissolve　—　seeing ourselves brought toward the point where, green no longer cutting though green, all absences are suspended or revoked.

— « je ne pourrai pas vivre dans un pays où il n'y a pas de silex. »

— « là, Pierre, émerge dans les terres lavées par l'orage jus-
qu'à la coupure de l'horizon, comme à la paume de la main
s'ajustera le temps, sur son tranchant l'amande de silex. »

— 'I couldn't live in a place where there's no flint.'

— 'there, Pierre, emerges from the lands washed by the storm all the way to the horizon's edge, just as time will shape itself to the palm of the hand, the kernel of flint on its cutting edge.'

Á l'arrêt

dehors

       mais vide
le dehors

aujourd'hui
entrailles et poumons
dans
le grand froid

à côté de la porte

comme un torchon accrochés

          passer
dehors

la neige n'a pas été écorchée

At a standstill

outside

       but empty
the outdoors

today
guts and lungs
in
the sharp chill

next to the door

they're hung up like a rag

                going
outside

the snow hasn't been skinned

mais dehors
           une bête à nouveau le dehors

et le croc du vide

au
déboulé

tête

               traversée encore
par ce qui plus loin
emportera

toi-même si tu as pu
parler

remuer
une fois encore

but outside
        an animal again the outdoors

and the fang of emptiness

at a
bolt

head

             crossed again
by what farther on
will carry away

yourself if you were able
to speak

stir
once again

                              à la neige
un instant ce souffle de
la neige

de son propre poids

            et comme un peu plus haut
alors

            accroché

              to the snow
an instant this breath of
snow

by its own weight

         and as a bit higher
then

     hung up

mais

            dehors
        sans l'avoir
arrêté

je ne peux pas

comme

        avalanche
de l'air
ressurgi

but

                                        outside
                        without having
stopped it

I cannot

reemerged

                        as
avalanche
of the air

tu as
        accroché
le
véloce

          immobile
animal des mots

         emporte

you have

            hung up

the

rapid

            motionless

animal of words

        carries off

plaqué à terre

        peu après
en pièces

comme entre terre et soi
                la neige

par plaque
        et plaque enfuies

patched to earth

       shortly after
in pieces

as between earth and itself
           the snow

patch by
       patch fled

le dehors

le
tout petit

du dehors lui-même comme l'autre jour une
                                        bête
sorti   et ressorti

tu avances

cela
n'a pas bougé

the outdoors

the very
smallest

of the outdoors itself as the other day an
                                        animal
came out   and came out again

you move forward

that
has not budged

André du Bouchet: The Silence Outside

André du Bouchet's commitment to art issues from a long tradition. Among French writers, poets in particular have dedicated far more attention to the visual arts than their counterparts in our language, despite a few recent exceptions like Frank O'Hara or John Ashbery. In the nineteenth century, Baudelaire, who is often considered the father of modern art-criticism, wrote extensively on Delacroix, the various Salons, and humor in the arts. Mallarmé crafted jewel-like "medallions" of Whistler, Manet, and Morisot; with Renoir, he was photographed by Degas. In our time, these poets' successors have allied themselves with visual artists even more closely—not only through their essays on art, but also through collaborations melding the graphic and the verbal, such as art-books or portfolios of engravings, accompanied by full-blown texts. Du Bouchet was a leading proponent of this trend, and he shared his enthusiasm with the co-founders of *L'Éphémère*, the journal he edited in the late sixties and early seventies with Yves Bonnefoy and Jacques Dupin, among others.

In its pages, all three poets focused on the visual arts almost as much as on literature, just as they did throughout their lives. As a young man, du Bouchet served as an assistant to the art historian, Georges Duthuit, then at work on *Le feu des signes*, his magnum opus. Du Bouchet went on to compose elusive disquisitions on art in his own right, in a uniquely elliptical style. Like Dupin and Bonnefoy, he especially revered Giacometti; but he also wrote about many other contemporary artists, such as Pierre Tal Coat and Bram Van Velde, or figures from the past such as Nicolas Poussin and Hercules Seghers. Dupin, who was the friend of Joan Miró and Francis Bacon as well as Giacometti, produced a large corpus of works on the visual arts; for many years he served as the director of publications at the prestigious Galerie Maeght, which sponsored *L'Éphémère*. As for Bonnefoy, his books on art such as *L'Arrière-Pays* and *Rome, 1630* are key to grasping the frequent allusions to Renaissance and Baroque paintings in his poems.

While the cross-fertilization between art and poetry is obvious in Dupin and Bonnefoy, du Bouchet takes it a step further, into the realm of technique. His second wife's father, Nicolas de Staël, was a celebrated painter; the poet's son, Gilles du Bouchet, has pursued a distinguished career in the visual arts. In the latter's studio, and those of many friends over the years, André du Bouchet had ample occasion to view artists at work. While critics normally separate painterly methods from poetic devices, in his writings they constantly fuse. As we read the two longest texts in the present collection, "Taking flight" and "Notes on translation," a familiar word crops up repeatedly—in an unfamiliar sense. I am referring to the term "support," used by artists to denote the basic material that undergirds their work, whether paper, canvas, steel, or a host of other supports. By analogy, du Bouchet asks us, what is the support of poetry? Language, we would be tempted to reply: but that response leads us quickly into a maze. There is syntax at work, as well as prosody, vocabulary, tone, metaphor, ideational stance, and so on; but as we advance from word to word, perhaps it is ultimately the silence between them that forms their support—or even the blank space on the page. Silences and blanks alter words; they are changed by words in turn. As we shift from language to language, in the process of translation, we realize that silences and blanks are polyglot, never the same in any given tongue. Speech colors the unspoken; the unsaid modulates speech.

To draw a correlation with music, the rests in Bach differ from those in Debussy: decisive and expectant, as opposed to fluid and suggestive. But within a single piece or even a brief passage by the same composer, silence will take on a thousand different nuances, according to the context. In "Taking flight," with startling refinement, du Bouchet analyses similar subtleties in the visual realm. He lets us see the work through his own eyes, but also through the mind and hand of the painter who is creating it—presumably his friend Tal Coat, cited in the epigraph. Readers of American poetry will recall the painter's association with Wallace Stevens, who owned a still-life by him; the canvas inspired his poem "Angel Surrounded by Paysans" (1950), which includes the often-quoted lines:

> I am the angel of reality,
> Seen for the moment standing in the door.
>
> I have neither ashen wing nor wear of ore
> And live without a tepid aureole,
>
> Or stars that follow me, not to attend,
> But, of my being and its knowing, part.
>
> I am one of you and being one of you
> Is being and knowing what I am and know.
>
> Yet I am the necessary angel of earth,
> Since, in my sight, you see the earth again...

It might seem that the measured chords of Stevens are as far-removed from the staccato fragments of du Bouchet as possible. However, from my first conversation with the author in Paris, I realized that he cultivated our English-language poets more than we ourselves, thanks to his eight years of literary studies at Loomis, Amherst, and Harvard—not to mention his youthful exchanges with James Merrill and Richard Wilbur. Not only did the striking phrase "the necessary angel" become the title of Stevens's principal book of essays, it also reveals an unexpected commonality between him and du Bouchet.

Clearly, the angel is poetry—but not, as in the Romantic concept, a spirit grander and more sublime than ordinary presences, whether beings or objects (in Tal Coat's still-life, the "angel" is a napkin and the "paysans" are articles of crockery). Here there are no "flashes that have shewn to us/ The invisible world," to quote Wordsworth. The stars do not attend poetry with celestial aspirations; they are subsumed into its essence and its knowledge, "since, in my sight, you see the earth again." The general precept set forth by Stevens sharpens to microscopic focus in du Bouchet, whether he describes his walks through nature, his thoughts on translation, or his reflections on art. In "Taking flight," the image of a flock of seagulls intrigues him less than the artist's placing of dots and lines on the support.

naked paper furnishes the background.

the fraction of globe we pace out
offers but a face, at each glance, that is once more effaced.

crossed.   it's the background that's crossed.   it's the background
that crosses.

In effect, at every moment we ourselves are moving like marks across paper, and our supporting medium is the world itself, which streams through our consciousness just as it rolls through time and space. Here we encounter the "this in which" of George Oppen's poetry—and indeed, of all profoundly attuned awareness. There is no room for self-obsessed feeling in du Bouchet's drama of description: contemplating the grandeur of nature, he goes out to meet it, merging the physical universe with the ever-expanding canvas of the mind. As John Taylor comments: "An immediate authoritativeness emanates from this oeuvre that can seem austere and obliquely styled, although its aim is to bring us—jar us—into contact with the simplest, the most rudimentary, aspects of reality."

Du Bouchet authored many essays on art, some of them book-length; for example, he published a major work with his son, Gilles, tersely entitled *Peinture* (*Painting*, 1983). He fostered a constant interplay of verbal and visual expression, which disregarded the usual boundaries. Within literature, he practiced a similar blurring of distinctions, passing effortlessly from poetry to prose and back again. Under his hand, aesthetic categories mutated as quickly as images; to paraphrase Ezra Pound, he "wove an endless metaphor."

Not surprisingly, given his passion for shifting shapes, he produced audacious translations from the English, Russian, and German. He was known for pushing the envelope of languages—more concerned with catching the overtones of words than hair-splitting their definitions. As he fully recognized, he sometimes engaged in delicate balancing acts; yet he maintained that the only "exact" translation is to copy out the text just as it is, without attempting to render it into another tongue. He followed Walter Benjamin in praising Hölderlin's versions of Pindar and Sophocles as the acme of translation—from within rather than without. As with artworks, he was more focused on the "supporting medium" of languages than on the individual words, no matter how minutely he examined them. In his poetry as well, phrases leap across spaces on a page or intervals in speech, unveiling what stands behind, above, and beneath them. In this sense, each language is a mega-word, connected to others by a series of hiatuses, and lapsing back into silence once more. That conviction lies at the core of "Notes on translation":

> torrential matter,
> and, at first sight, not having moved, which — quicker than the
> words of the language, has been the words' support.

> from its temporary support, the word has incorporated
> something even — remaining open then, has discovered itself
> caught off guard. like oneself, road, paper.

> lending an ear
> to what the road hasn't conveyed, what the word hasn't been able
> to say.
> on an interrupted expectancy, since the
> language will find its body in an expectancy, I've — without
> sustaining it then, attained what is
> beyond the language.

Though du Bouchet naturally required that translations should be "faithful to the originals," he invited readers to see the semantic disjunctions between one language and another as opportunities rather than defects. Like the volley of impressions coming our way from nature, the "torrential matter" of any language as used by native speakers keeps them from apprehending the silence that underpins it. If poetry is the "necessary angel" that allows us to "see the earth anew," and if art is the set of strokes that brings out the background, then translation is the medium that permits us to break through all languages, to rediscover the wordlessness of a "this in which" far more substantive than speech: the world "outside," beyond ourselves.

"Outside" ("dehors") is a term that frequently recurs in du Bouchet's writing: it signifies the absence of the human, the wide horizon of the uninhabited outdoors, the staggering vastnesses of stellar space. In his poetry, du Bouchet strives to encompass those distances, to expose us to their primal, metamorphic forces. The contradiction inherent to such a desire is that we can only divine the "outside" from within our minds, through the lens of the senses or the deductions of thought, both equally unreliable. As du Bouchet concludes in what was probably his final poem, "At a standstill":

outside

without having

stopped it

I cannot

reemerged

as

avalanche
of the air

you have

hung up
the
rapid

motionless
animal of words

In a typically taut yet open-ended design—as much visual as verbal— du Bouchet draws together the principal threads of his lifelong quest for truth, no matter how daunting that truth may be. The paradox of poetry is that unless it ceases to speak, the fecund silence toward which it tends cannot enter into play: the poet cannot go "outside without having stopped it." What he was seeking reemerges as the world itself, the crushing "avalanche of air" that takes his breath away. He hangs up his vain attempt to approach it like a hollow pelt;

language, which seemed so "rapid," is now the "motionless animal of words." The poem is always a betrayal of nature, a kind of taxidermy. But innate to the ceaseless hunt for meaning is the wildness that escapes us. Killing the vital language we love, freezing it into the trophies we call poems, we arrive at an inkling of what awaits us beyond them. We have gained what far surpasses any Romantic reverie: reality itself.

As Oppen—invoking Heidegger—reminds us, we must wend our way along "the arduous path of appearance." This is a mystical path, no doubt, but one where detachment rejoins attachment. In an early essay on du Bouchet, his friend Bonnefoy identified the crux of his work:

> Because André du Bouchet only demands soberness, tightness, and silence from his words, it is sometimes thought that he harbors an attraction towards nothingness and emptiness… His poetry is not an eradication of subjectivity, any more than a refusal of sensuous richness, but rather a denial of their degraded elements… If he persists in wandering, in the solitude of presence, "around this gleam"—since founding anything remains forever difficult—this will still be truth to the utmost. To any future existence, the work of André du Bouchet already offers its exemplary energy, its inexhaustible wellspring of transformations. And there are few in our time who embody so decisively that outer limit our age must reach: the purity of the poetic act.

As atoms spin through micro-space—and galaxies, macro-space—words wheel through the interstices that both divide and link them. Du Bouchet's writing rejects nothing—even nothing itself; it is not ascetic, but all-embracing, just as absence and presence, death and life perpetually intertwine. In his multi-faceted poetry, every line—and every gap—lays bare the blankness that permeates art, the unsayable that haunts translation, and the silence that engenders speech.

—Hoyt Rogers

Source Notes

Introduction

All translations by Eric Fishman, with the exception of Hoyt Rogers's translations of du Bouchet. For excerpts from poems contained in this volume, the poem title and page number are given below.

xi   "Upright on great sediments...": "A thing..." p. 177.

xi   Yves Bonnefoy, "La poésie d'André du Bouchet," in *Critique*, April 1962, pp. 291-298.

xi   "It's now a matter ..." André du Bouchet, *Aveuglante ou banale, essais sur la poésie (1949–1959)*, Clément Layet et François Tison, eds. (Paris : Le Bruit du temps, 2011), pp. 143–44.

xi   "The mountain in *reality*...": "1966," p. 121.

xi   "Like the field...": "The Journey," p. 67.

xii   Description of du Bouchet's "sculptural" techniques: Clément Layet. *André du Bouchet*. (Paris: Seghers, 2002).

xii   "My poems run ceaselessly...": "Notebook fragments, 1952-1954," p. 41.

xii   "Poppies, / the red harvest...": "Poppies..." p. 169.

xii   "Eye / a switchblade": "Motor of night," p. 23.

xii   "Across from me...": "Jubilation..." p. 179.

xiii   "The muffled, crackling breath...": "Skidding on a patch of ice, snow's waste," p. 117.

xiii   "The sentence is shattered": "Skidding on a patch of ice, snow's waste," p. 115.

xiii   "*Rauschen*..." and "in language...": "1971," p. 135.

xiii   "Keep something of...": "Notes on translation," p. 91.

xiv   "I translated...": "Notes on Translation," p. 89.

xi-xiv   Additional sources: *L'Étrangère*, double volume "André du Bouchet," 2007; *Europe*: *Revue littéraire mensuelle*, special edition "André du Bouchet," 2011; Hoyt Rogers, "The Restless Openwork of André du Bouchet," in *Openwork*, translated by Paul Auster and Hoyt Rogers (New Haven: Yale University Press [Margellos Series], 2014).

Poetry and prose by André du Bouchet

Une lampe dans la lumière aride: carnets 1949-1955 (*A Lamp in the Arid Light: Notebooks 1949-1955*), edited by Clément Layet. Paris: Le Bruit du temps, 2011.
    « Valse / Marine » (from a notebook entry dated June 1949)
    « La chrysalide … » (September/October 1949) •
    « Le rôle des mots » (September/October 1949) •
    « Moteur de la nuit » (July 1950)
    « Répétition » (April 1951) •
    "Notebook fragments, April 1951" ○
    « Une vache qui tousse dans la brume … » (August 15, 1951) •
    « La ville, le champ, brûle sans bruit… » (August 16, 1951) •+
    « Aube sans soleil … » (August 1951) •
    « La buée étouffe doucement la vue … » (October 1951) •
    « Et je puis dire que mon orgueil … » (November 1952) •
    "Notebook fragments, 1952-1954" ○

Air, suivi de Défets: 1950-1953 (*Air, followed by Loose Pages: 1950-1953*) Fontfroide-le-Haut: Fata Morgana, 1986.
    « En aval »
    « La terre »
    « Vu »
    « La préhistoire »
    « Varengeville »
    « Points de chute »
    « Élargissement »
    « Nature sèche »

Le moteur blanc (*The White Motor*). Paris: GLM, 1956.
    « Autre resort »

Botteghe oscure, vol. 18, Fall 1956.
    « Le voyage »

Dans la chaleur vacante (*In the Vacant Heat*). Paris: Mercure de France, 1961.
    « Avant que la blancheur »

Où le soleil (*Where the Sun*). Paris: Mercure de France, 1968.
    « Solstice »
    « La terre … »
    « Avant le matin »

L'incohérence (*Incoherence*). Paris: Hachette, 1979. [Reprint, Fata Morgana, 1984].
    « Porteur d'un livre dans la montagne »

Ici en deux (*Here in Two*). Paris: Mercure de France, 1986.
    « Notes sur la traduction » •

Une tache (*A Stain*). Fontfroide-le-Haut: Fata Morgana, 1988.
    « Dérapage sur une plaque de verglas, déchet de la neige » •

Carnet 2 (*Notebook 2*). Fontfroide-Le-Haut: Fata Morgana, 1998.
    « 1966 » •
    « 1968 » •
    « 1970 » •
    « 1971 » •

L'ajour (*Openwork*). Paris: Gallimard, 1998.
    « Congère »
    « Luzerne »
    « L'asphalte »

Annotations sur l'espace non-datées, Carnet 3 (*Undated Annotations on Space, Notebook 3*).
Fontfroide-Le-Haut: Fata Morgana, 2000. **
    « Ca – va – lari – a – a – a – na … »
    « Coqulicots … »
    « Alors que je passe … »
    « Langage n'attend pas… »
    « Une chose … »
    « Jubilation … »

L'emportement du muet (*The Rage of the Mute*). Paris: Mercure de France, 2000.
    « Essor » •
    « Deux traces vertes » •

Tumulte (*Tumult*). Saint-Clément-la-Rivière: Fata Morgana, 2001.
    « À l'arret »

• These selections have been distilled from their original length, as discussed in the introduction.

** Since the volume comprises one continuous text, these are excerpts.

+ The notebook entry may refer to a mysterious case of mass poisoning in the small town of Pont-Saint-Esprit on August 15th, 1951.

º Fragments selected and assembled by Eric Fishman.

Afterword

All translations by Hoyt Rogers. Besides the "Introduction" sources cited above, such as the essay by Yves Bonnefoy, please see:

George Oppen, *This in Which* (1965), epigraph by Martin Heidegger, in *New Collected Poems* (New Directions, 2008), ed. Michael Davidson, p. 92.

Wallace Stevens, *The Collected Poems* (Knopf, 1954), p. 496.
—*The Necessary Angel: Essays on Reality and the Imagination* (Knopf, 1951).

John Taylor, "In Quest of the Elemental—André du Bouchet's *Openwork*," in *Arts Fuse,* October 13, 2014.

About the Poet and Translators

André du Bouchet (1924–2001) is recognized as one of the greatest French authors of the twentieth century. A groundbreaking poet, he was also a prolific translator from the English, German, and Russian, as well as a noted critic of art and literature. He published nearly seventy books in all. These include scores of volumes of verse and lyric prose, numerous works on Giacometti and other artists, along with translations of Faulkner, Shakespeare, Joyce, Hölderlin, Riding, and Pasternak. In the late sixties he co-founded—with Yves Bonnefoy, Jacques Dupin, Paul Celan, and others—the influential literary journal *L'Éphémère*. Among many honors, he was awarded the National Poetry Prize of France in 1983.

—

Eric Fishman is an educator, writer, and translator. He studied English literature and translation at Yale, and French literature at the University of Paris. He is currently translating a collection of poetry by Monchoachi, one of the major contemporary poets of Martinique. Along with other editors, he recently founded a magazine of poetry and art by young people. For more about his work, please see ericjpfishman.com.

—

Hoyt Rogers is a writer and translator. His poems, stories, and essays have appeared in a wide variety of periodicals. He translates from the French, German, Italian, and Spanish; he has translated books by Bonnefoy and Borges, among many other authors. With Paul Auster, he published *Openwork*, the first anthology of du Bouchet in English. For further information, please visit hoytrogers.com.

THE BITTER OLEANDER PRESS
Library of Poetry

TRANSLATION SERIES

Torn Apart by Joyce Mansour —translated by Serge Gavronsky
(France)

Children of the Quadrilateral by Benjamin Péret —translated by Jane Barnard
(France) & Albert Frank Moritz

Edible Amazonia by Nicomedes Suárez-Araúz —translated by Steven Ford Brown
(Bolivia)

A Cage of Transparent Words by Alberto Blanco —a bilingual edition with multiple translators
(Mexico)

Afterglow by Alberto Blanco —translated by Jennifer Rathbun
(Mexico)

Of Flies and Monkeys by Jacques Dupin —translated by John Taylor
(France)

1001 Winters by Kristiina Ehin —translated by Ilmar Lehtpere
(Estonia)

Tobacco Dogs by Ana Minga —translated by Alexis Levitin
(Ecuador)

Sheds by José-Flore Tappy * —translated by John Taylor
(Switzerland)

Puppets in the Wind by Karl Krolow —translated by Stuart Friebert
(Germany)

Movement Through the End by Philippe Rahmy —translated by Rosemary Lloyd
(Switzerland)

Ripened Wheat: Selected Poems of Hai Zi ** —translated by Ye Chun
(China)

Confetti-Ash: Selected Poems of Salvador Novo —translated by Anthony Seidman
(Mexico) & David Shook

Territory of Dawn: Selected Poems of Eunice Odio —translated by Keith Ekiss, Sonia P. Ticas
(Costa Rica) & Mauricio Espinoza

The Hunchbacks' Bus by Nora Iuga *** —translated by Adam J. Sorkin
(Romania) & Diana Manole

To Each Unfolding Leaf: Selected Poems (1976-2015) by Pierre Voélin
(Switzerland) —translated by John Taylor

Shatter the Bell in My Ear by Christine Lavant
(Austria) —translated by David Chorlton

The Little Book of Passage by Franca Mancinelli
(Italy) —translated by John Taylor

Forty-One Objects by Carsten René Nielsen
(Denmark) —translated by David Keplinger

At an Hour's Sleep from Here by Franca Mancinelli
(Italy) —translated by John Taylor

Outside by André du Bouchet
(France) —translated by Eric Fishman
& Hoyt Rogers

---

* Finalist for National Translation Award from American Literary Translators Association (ALTA)—2015
** Finalist for Lucien Stryk Asian Translation Award from American Literary Translators Association (ALTA)—2016
*** Long-Listed for National Translation Award from American Literary Translators Association (ALTA)—2017

ORIGINAL POETRY SERIES

* Winner of The Bitter Oleander Press Library of Poetry Award (BOPLOPA)
** Utah Book Award Winner (2012)
*** Typography, Graphic Design & Poetry

All back issues and single copies of *The Bitter Oleander* are available for $10.00
For more information, contact us at info@bitteroleander.com
Visit us on Facebook or www.bitteroleander.com

The font used in this book is the digital representation of a family of type developed by William Caslon (1692-1766). Printer Benjamin Franklin introduced Caslon into the American colonies, where it was used extensively, including the official printing of The Declaration of Independence by a Baltimore printer. Caslon's fonts have a variety of design, giving them an uneven, rhythmic texture that adds to their visual interest and appeal. The Caslon foundry continued under his heirs and operated until the 1960s.